JACK INK

Pregnancy Book for Dads

The Complete Guide to Pregnancy, Childbirth, Postpartum & Fatherhood

This book was professionally typeset on Reedsy.
Find out more at reedsy.com

Contents

Foreword

As a married man and first-time father, I'm here to help you prepare for the monumental challenge of pregnancy and parenthood that lies ahead. It won't be easy, but it will certainly be worth it!

Rather than seeing yourself as a "coach" or "supportive wife," think of yourself as the husband of the woman you fell in love with.

Congratulations, your family is about to become a little bigger! I'm not an expert, so don't expect me to be one. But I've got some helpful advice from my personal experience that might make life a little easier when the baby arrives.

Let's start with patience - above all else, make sure you have patience with her! You'll probably have to take classes together and read up on different aspects of newborn care - but that's all part of the journey. Embrace it.

After all, you chose this life together. And believe me; there are some truly amazing moments ahead that you'll never forget!

Jack Ink

Acknowledgement

Writing this book has been a journey filled with invaluable insights and learning experiences, and I owe a great deal of gratitude to the people who made it all possible.

First, I would like to thank all the first-time dads and moms who generously shared their stories, wisdom, and challenges with me. Your honesty and willingness to share your experiences have made this book possible.

I also want to express my deepest appreciation to my family, friends, and loved ones who provided unwavering support, encouragement, and inspiration throughout the writing process. Your love and belief in me kept me going, and I am grateful for every word of encouragement you gave.

Finally, I thank my partner for being my rock throughout this journey. Your unwavering support, patience, and love have been the driving force behind this book, and I am forever grateful for everything you do.

To all the first-time dads and moms out there, I hope this book serves as a helpful guide on your journey, and I am honored to be a part of your lives.

Chapter 1

My wife and I have been on a steep learning curve from daily diaper changes to sleepless nights. But throughout this journey, I've discovered some valuable insights I want to share with other new dads.

Full disclosure, I am not a medical professional, nor do I have any formal education in postpartum care. Instead, my helpful advice comes from trial and error, learning from other dads, and a whole lot of research. I've made my fair share of mistakes and learned what works and doesn't.

This book is not a one-size-fits-all solution but a collection of my lessons. As a new dad, I know how overwhelming and confusing the postpartum period can be. This guide is designed to help dads navigate this transformative period with confidence and support.

My book offers practical tips on managing sleep deprivation, prioritizing self-care, assisting with breastfeeding, recognizing and managing postpartum depression, communicating and strengthening your relationship, and becoming a confident and supportive father.

Through personal stories and anecdotes, I share the ups and downs of my journey, highlighting the lessons I've learned along the way. I understand that every family is unique, and what works for me may not work for everyone. But I believe that by sharing our experiences, we can learn from each other and become better dads.

So if you're a new dad or about to become one, I invite you to join me on this journey. Let's navigate the unknown together and help each other become the best possible fathers we can be.

As a new father, I always wanted to hold my child in my arms someday.

And when my wife gave birth to our son eight weeks ago, I was filled with a mix of overwhelming joy and fear at the same time.

Every day was a new learning experience, and being a first-time father came with unique challenges. I had moments where I had no idea what I was doing, but I was doing my best to learn and grow as a parent. My wife and I took turns waking up throughout the night to feed and change our son, and the lack of sleep was one of our biggest challenges.

Caring for a baby was also messier than I had ever imagined. As someone who values tidiness, I quickly learned there was no room for perfection regarding diaper changes and spit-up. But amidst the mess and chaos, something was endearing in how my son relied on me and my wife for everything.

One of the most unexpected lessons I learned as a new father was how much becoming a parent taught me about my parents. The sacrifices they made for me over the years suddenly became crystal clear, and I felt grateful for everything they had done for me. While parenting isn't easy, I was so blessed to be able to carry on the love and care of my child.

As my son grows, I've realized that being a father is more than just cuddles and cute baby clothes. It's about being there for him through thick and thin, teaching him the value of hard work and the importance of family, and giving him a happy and healthy childhood filled with love and laughter.

Sometimes, when I hold my son in my arms, and he's dozing off to sleep, the world seems to slow down, and all that matters is the bond between us. I know there is still so much to learn and discover about being a father, but there's also a lifetime of joy and love to experience.

Watching him develop his unique personality and begin to explore the world around him fills me with pride and wonder. Being a parent comes with struggles and obstacles, but I truly believe that the rewards outweigh any difficulties.

As a first-time father, there are times when I feel overwhelmed or uncertain, but those moments are outweighed by the sense of joy and fulfillment that being a parent brings. My son is the light of my life, and I feel so lucky to be his dad. Parenthood isn't always easy, but it is one of the greatest adventures I've ever experienced.

As my son grew older, new challenges began to arise. One of the most difficult things for me was balancing my work life with my responsibilities as a father. It was a constant juggling act, and sometimes I felt like I wasn't doing enough in either area.

One of the biggest struggles that my wife and I faced as first-time parents was dealing with our fears and anxieties. It's natural to worry about the safety and well-being of your child, but it can be hard to shake those feelings and not let them consume you.

But as my son continued to grow and thrive, I found that my confidence as a father grew as well. Seeing him develop into a happy and healthy child gave me a sense of reassurance. The moments of frustration and exhaustion were always outweighed by the joy and love that came with being a parent.

I've also realized the importance of seeking advice and support from other parents. Whether it's a friend who has gone through similar experiences or attending parenting classes, having a community of people to turn to for guidance and support can be invaluable.

The journey of becoming a first-time father has been both challenging and rewarding. It's taught me the meaning of unconditional love and provided me with a renewed appreciation for my parents. While there have been struggles along the way, they've all been worth it to see my son grow and thrive into the amazing little boy he is today.

From learning how to read your baby's cues to understanding different stages within the first year, you'll be able to provide your little ones with the safe and supportive environment they need to thrive. You'll also receive straightforward explanations about common parenting issues and tips on making the most of your new role.

Plus, gain insight into what it means to take on such an important responsibility and set expectations for yourself as a father - all while cherishing the priceless moments that come with parenthood. This book is written especially for men and their unique parenting experiences.

Through empathy from other dads and a source of compassion, find out that you're not alone in this journey! With the guidance provided here, make mistakes and learn along the way, then turn those lessons into valuable pieces of wisdom to share with others.

So explore these pages before welcoming your newborn into your life – and don't forget, even though it may be intimidating initially, parenting has so many joys waiting for you around every corner!

Parenting is an amazing journey filled with love, joy, and magic - but it also comes with its challenges.

As a first-time dad, it's important to be aware of parenthood's potential dangers and surprises and the many helpful tips available to make the most of this experience.

With this book in hand, you'll be equipped to take on all aspects of your new role – from understanding cues your baby gives you to learning different stages within their first year and establishing healthy boundaries while cherishing every moment together!

So before you welcome your little one into the world, read this invaluable guide – and don't forget: when someone says "Danger Will Robinson! Danger!" They may just be trying to help!

Chapter 2

Feel Free To Ask For Help

It is easy to forget that asking for help is okay - but it is! You can bounce ideas off of a friend or reach out to someone you respect to get advice, and you may be surprised and even inspired by the feedback you receive.

So don't be afraid to ask for help when needed because it can lead to personal growth and new possibilities! It might seem unsafe sometimes, but opening it to others can improve your life in many ways.

Be Prepared For Sleepless Nights

When it comes to new parenthood, it is always a smart idea to be prepared for sleepless nights. Trust me, your little one will have their schedule, and you won't always catch a wink when the sun sets.

Unfortunately, all those late nights can take their toll on you, don't worry, though. There are steps you can take to help keep pace. Do your best to stay organized and on top of any house chores so you can relax when it's time for bed.

Working off a plan for you and your wife is key, too, as both of you need to stay well-rested to parents effectively! Lastly, accept that sometimes even with preparation, sleep might still be hard to come by — being prepared gives us the best shot at making sure everyone is comfortable and happy no matter what hour it is.

Your Life Will Change - For the Better!

There is no denying that life can be difficult at times, but beauty and magic are also in everything. We often do not realize how much our lives will change when we make positive steps forward.

We open the door to new opportunities when we step outside our comfort zone, face our fears, and work hard for what we want.

Whether that means taking a different path at work or investing in yourself through learning and self-development, life promises us so much more if we are willing to take risks and follow our hearts. Friend, your life will change - for the better!

Get Ready To Do A Lot Of Laundry

Doing laundry can be a chore, but it doesn't have to be the worst part of your day. To make the process smoother, start by gathering all your dirty items into a single place - an overflowing clothes basket or an overstuffed closet shelf.

Once you have everything together, it's time to separate colors, whites, and any delicate things that need hand washing. Before you toss in the detergent, double-check for any stains on your clothing and pre-treat if needed. Doing so will ensure that your clothes look clean and smell fresh each time!

You will Never Look At Poop the Same Way

Finding a new appreciation for something as unsavory as the poop is not easy, but that's exactly what you'll get.

You'll soon be scooping, cleaning, and monitoring all kinds of dookie! From the liquid newborn poop at 2 am to the stinker toddler version to the occasional surprise that comes after meals.

It's not always glamorous, but parenting changes your perspective on certain things - especially when it comes to poop. But they do not worry. You'll always have a wife in crime - your beloved diaper-changing station!

Say Goodbye to Your Social Life...For Now

Saying goodbye to your social life can be tough, especially if you are used to going out with friends almost every night or attending large gatherings over the weekend. It's natural to experience a sense of loss as we adjust to staying at home and navigating through a new normal.

However, it's important to remember that this situation is only temporary.

Eventually, life will return to how it was, and you will be able to reclaim the social life you had before this all began. But for now, enjoy the peace of spending time alone at home and getting lost in your hobbies playing guitar, doing puzzles, watching funny cat videos on YouTube just let yourself find joy in the things that make you happy when you're by yourself.

So there you have it, folks - the six things you need to know before becoming a parent. It's a wild ride, but it's so worth it.

Every moment is precious, even (or maybe especially) the tough ones. If you're considering taking the plunge into parenthood, go for it - and remember to ask for help when needed.

Adjust Your Expectations

As you adjust to this new role as a first-time dad, it's important to take your time and understand that you will only be perfect after a while.

Try to set realistic expectations and have patience with yourself. This can include setting reasonable goals for yourself, such as getting more sleep or carving out time for self-care.

It can also include communicating openly with your wife and family members who may be helping you through the transition of being a new parent.

It can also help to remember that making mistakes is part of the learning process - and that's okay! It's normal while learning to navigate all the changes that come with being a first-time dad.

As long as you stay aware of your limitations and practice self-compassion, you'll find it much easier to control your emotions in trying times.

Finally, understanding the support system is key at this stage! Be bold and lean on family, friends, or even healthcare professionals who have already been through all this before. Access to a person or resource that can provide advice when things get tough might save the day when everything feels overwhelming!

Keep Your Home Baby Safe

One of the most important tasks for first-time parents before their baby arrives is ensuring their home is safe and secure. This involves using child-proofing gadgets and devices and being mindful about the items that are kept within the baby's reach.

Common household items such as cleaning supplies, tools, and sharp objects should all be kept away from your little one! By creating a safe environment for your child to explore, you can rest assured that potential dangers are kept out of sight.

This can include putting valuable items in locked closets or cabinets, storing medication in a locked drawer or cabinet, and placing safety locks on doors or drawers where hazardous materials may be present.

Additionally, you can use special corner guards to protect furniture corners, determine which outlets need covers and ensure windows are closed tightly with blinds or curtains so that curious babies won't climb up!

Lastly, check on these items regularly throughout your baby's growth and development stages, as it's easy for danger zones to change over time. By creating a safe environment for your child, you'll have peace of mind knowing that your family will be well taken care of!

The Basics of Infant Nutrition and Clothing

Regarding your baby's nutrition and clothing, it's important to ensure they have everything they need to grow and develop at a healthy rate. A basic understanding of the necessary vitamins and minerals and the types of clothing best for newborns can help set your little one up for success!

When it comes to their diet, you'll want to ensure their meals are balanced with proteins, carbohydrates, fruits, and vegetables - as these will provide them with key nutrients for growth.

As far as clothing goes, you'll want to stick with lightweight materials that can better regulate their temperature in warmer or colder climates. By researching infant nutrition and clothing basics, you can help ensure your baby gets the nourishment and comfort they need!

You know what type of nutrition is best for your baby's needs. If you have any questions or concerns, always consult your pediatrician.

Breastmilk is a great source of nutrition; plenty of quality formulas are available if you need more than that. Additionally, if you plan on choosing solid foods for your infant down the line, you'll want to make sure they are age-appropriate foods to ensure their safety and proper nutrient absorption. For clothing, light layers are the most comfortable and safe.

It's especially important to remember things like socks and booties during colder months when trying to keep your little one warm. Hats should also be used if your baby is in direct sunlight - newborns can burn quickly without protection!

Lastly, it's key that all clothes are washed before use due to their sensitive skin - so always choose gentle detergents that won't irritate delicate skin. With the right understanding of infant nutrition and clothing basics, you can help give your little one the best start from day one!

Raising a child is no easy feat, and self-care is an incredibly important aspect of parenting. Taking the time to nurture personal relationships with your wife or other loved ones can help you find solace in your new role as a parent.

Having a strong support system will not only benefit both parents but will also help foster a healthier environment for their children. As parents, it's important to remember that taking care of yourself and finding moments of joy throughout this journey is essential for maintaining balance and staying positive.

Whether it's taking an evening off to relax with friends and family, planning regular dates with your significant other, or just finding some quiet time to yourself - remember that taking care of your physical and mental well-being should always be a priority.

Prioritize Self-Care and Relationships

Parenting can be challenging, and it is important to remember that leaning on your wife or other loved ones can help you stay strong during difficult times.

Consider scheduling regular date nights with your significant other, allowing both parents to recharge and reconnect. If parenting takes up most of your free time, take advantage of family support systems such as grandparents, siblings, or friends willing to provide short-term childcare when needed.

If you don't have access to local family support, consider contacting trusted neighbors or investigating hiring a professional babysitter for extra help around the house.

Spending money on childcare might seem daunting, but providing some much-needed respite can work wonders in helping reduce stress levels and allow parents to enjoy quality time together.

Fears of Being a First-Time Dad

Being a first-time dad is an experience unlike any other. The journey of parenthood is full of excitement and anticipation but also fear and uncertainty.

It can feel overwhelming to figure out how to be the best father you can be for your child, especially if you are a first-time dad with no previous experience raising a child. Fortunately, there are plenty of resources out there to help guide new dads through this uncharted territory.

Before your new family member arrives, it's important to take some time to prepare yourself for such a big life change mentally. Figure out what parenting style works best for you and your wife.

Think about everything that's going to change—from having less free time and less sleep to dealing with late-night feedings, diaper changes, or temper tantrums—and know it's all part of the process.

Additionally, don't be afraid to reach out for support from family, friends, and healthcare professionals who have already been through all this before. With patience and dedication, being a first-time dad can be an exciting and rewarding experience for everyone involved!

Before Your Little One Arrives

It is important for couples expecting a child to discuss several topics before the baby arrives. These topics include finances, increased stress levels, and parenting roles. Establishing expectations can lead to a smoother transition into parenthood and help ensure both parents feel supported and adequately prepared when their little one finally arrives.

Challenges That Fathers Face

Fathers face unique parenting challenges that can often be difficult to navigate. As the breadwinner and protectors of their families, fathers may feel pressured to provide for their children's every need.

Fathers must also learn how to differentiate between taking on traditional roles and new ones created by a changing social landscape.

Additionally, as men increasingly become more involved in their children's lives, they may need clarification about how to tackle traditionally handled by mothers, such as feeding, bathing, and putting their children down for sleep.

Furthermore, with the increased number of working fathers in the workforce today, many worry about balancing work with parenting duties which can lead to guilt or anxiety. Fathers must find support to cope better with these unique challenges.

Fathers must also try to remain connected and build strong relationships with their children. The bond between father and child is one of the most important aspects of raising a healthy, well-adjusted individual.

Studies have repeatedly shown that fathers who are emotionally close to their children often have more secure and successful adults.

Fathers should be actively involved in their children's lives, participating in activities such as family dinners, playing games or sports, attending school events, and participating in special bonding activities like plays, outings, or even spending time alone with the baby.

By creating a meaningful connection, fathers can ensure that they remain present in their children's lives even when work or other commitments may limit their ability to do so.

Fathers also need to learn how to be both a disciplinarian and friends. Setting boundaries is important for children as it allows them to understand what is expected of them and reinforces the fact that their values and opinions are respected.

Fathers must remember, however, that discipline should not just be about punishment but also teaching appropriate behavior to help their children grow into responsible adults.

While setting boundaries, fathers should also make friends with their kids by engaging in fun activities or simply listening to their stories to provide emotional support when needed. By striking the right balance between discipline and friendship, fathers can successfully guide their children through many challenges.

Boundaries are important for fathers because they help guide their children's behavior and ensure they understand their expectations.

Setting limits also helps to reinforce values such as respect and responsibility while helping to create stability in the home. Clear boundaries also give children a sense of security, knowing that there are certain expectations they must meet to maintain peace and harmony within the family.

Most importantly, boundaries allow fathers to show their children they are respected and loved by setting consistent limits and expressing their love through thoughtful actions.

Chapter 3

Father-child relationships can be an important source of comfort, guidance, and learning opportunities for children. Fathers provide a unique perspective on life and the world that can shape their child's views and beliefs.

They show love and affection by spending quality time together, engaging in sports, playing board games, or going out for ice cream.

From a young age, fathers can teach their kids values like respect, responsibility, honesty, and hard work, which will stay with them for the rest of their lives.

Taking the time to listen to their children and showing them an appreciation for who they are—not what they achieve—will create a strong bond between father and son/daughter that can last a lifetime.

Quality time is a vital component of any relationship and involves more than just spending time together. Quality time focuses on creating meaningful experiences with one another that promote connection and understanding.

This could involve anything from a shared interest, such as a hobby or sport, to having an open conversation about your thoughts and feelings.

Quality time can also be simply being present with someone and letting them know they are valued without needing words.

The key to quality time is minimizing distractions by ensuring space for the two of you to truly engage in quality interactions, free from judgment or assumptions.

Active listening is an important skill to have in any meaningful relationship. It involves actively engaging and focusing on the speaker, providing feedback through non-verbal cues, restating what has been said before responding, and maintaining eye contact.

As opposed to passive listening, active listening encourages a deeper understanding of the other person's opinion or feelings through empathetic communication.

It can be a powerful tool for resolving conflict in interpersonal dynamics, as it shows respect and a willingness to understand one another. This listening skill can benefit both individuals involved in a conversation, as it fosters mutual understanding and encourages further dialogue.

Active listening can be an invaluable tool to support your wife during and after her delivery. You can provide a comforting and supportive presence that demonstrates respect for your wife's feelings and opinions by actively engaging in the conversation.

You can better understand her needs through active communication and offer timely assistance or advice whenever necessary. You can also tell her feelings are valid, reassuring her that she is not alone in this experience.

Showing empathy through active listening will help ease any stress or worry your wife may be feeling about a delivery, helping to create a strong bond between the two of you during this special moment in both of your lives.

New fatherhood can be challenging and overwhelming, but it doesn't mean there is less space for love and support. A husband can show his newborn and wife love and support by simply being present.

Being physically present during the transition can provide comfort in knowing you are there to take on any challenges. Expressing your love through words and actions will help show your commitment to the new family dynamic.

Show your wife appreciation for all her hard work during this special time in both of your lives and for giving tender, loving care to your newborn. This will help create a strong foundation you can continue building as a family.

Get Ready to Experience the Love

You are ready to embark on a life-changing journey of parenthood! The love, joy, and special moments you'll experience with your newborn are unparalleled.

Make sure to take full advantage of the quality time away from work and use it to make even more magical memories with your child. From outdoor adventures to sitting down for dinner meals, each moment will be something your family cherishes for years to come.

Recognizing the physical and emotional changes your wife will go through as she prepares to welcome a new life into her own is an important part of being supportive.

Your wife may experience dramatic hormonal shifts, extreme fatigue, cravings, aches and pains, morning sickness, mood swings, and more.

Understanding the effects of these changes can help you provide much-needed physical and emotional comfort for your spouse during the journey ahead. Every woman's experience with pregnancy is unique, but some common physical and emotional changes can be expected.

Your wife may experience drastic hormonal shifts, extreme fatigue, cravings, aches and pains, morning sickness, mood swings, and more. Additionally, she may feel anxious and uncertain about the many changes that come along with pregnancy. It's important to support your wife during this time of transition by understanding the effects of these changes and offering her comfort in any way you can.

- Research the changes she will experience.
- Talk to her about her feelings.
- Offer physical and emotional comfort.
- Assist with housework around the home.
- Help with any appointments or errands that need to be done.
- Show your love and understanding for your wife.
- Please educate yourself on the emotional, mental, and physical changes that could occur during her pregnancy.

- Provide a listening ear for your wife to express her fears or concerns.
- Comfort her with words of love and understanding.
- Offer practical ways to manage the physical changes, including exercising together, eating healthy meals, massages, and responsible use of medications.
- Spend quality time together without external distractions such as phones or television.
- Ask how you can help with errands such as grocery shopping or making appointments.
- Look into support groups in your area if needed.

Learn how to support your wife with the emotional, mental, and physical changes as she journeys through her pregnancy.

Brush Up on Your Conflict Resolution Skills

Becoming a father is an incredibly rewarding experience, but it can also be a difficult time of transition and adjustment. The relationship between you and your spouse can be heavily tested as you adjust to the new roles of parenthood.

Communication becomes even more important, and learning how to solve conflicts productively can make all the difference in maintaining a strong relationship during this time. This will explore the importance of communication, ways to invest in your marriage, and brushing up on conflict resolution skills for new fathers.

Maintaining open and honest communication with your wife is crucial to any healthy relationship, especially for new fathers and their wives. Good communication allows both parties to express their feelings respectfully and better understand each other's points of view.

Through thoughtful discussion, the couple can navigate life's inevitable conflicts more easily by taking the time to listen, understand, and work out solutions that can benefit both parties. This helps to ensure that all needs are met while building trust and deepening the bond in the relationship.

Investing in your marriage and relationship is one of the best things a couple can do to ensure a healthy and happy union.

According to experts, spending quality time together regularly, engaging in meaningful conversations, expressing appreciation for each other, practicing flexibility and compromise when differences arise, and incorporating humor into disagreements are important ways couples can invest in their relationship and strengthen the bond they share.

Showing affirmation towards one another can help create an atmosphere of understanding and support that will last over time.

Other action items couples can take to invest in their relationship include:

- Participating in activities together.
- Sharing intimate details about each other's lives.
- Avoiding criticism and blaming.
- Being patient with one another.
- Adjusting expectations as needed.
- Taking responsibility for their actions.

Additionally, couples should strive to set aside regular time to enjoy one another's company without any distractions or outside pressures. In these moments, a couple can connect in ways that make the relationship stronger and more meaningful.

Common pitfalls when a relationship is going sour due to the stress of a newborn can include criticism and blame, neglecting to prioritize time for each other, and communication breakdown. All couples face different challenges, especially when the stress of parenthood or other life changes enters the picture.

To help prevent the relationship from further deteriorating, couples should stay connected through dialogue about feelings, needs, and wants. Additionally, couples should strive to show understanding and patience with one another during stress and practice forgiveness when either wife slips up.

Different approaches to difficult conversations include staying calm, setting boundaries, expressing feelings without attacking the other person, and being open to compromise.

It is important to focus on communication that is respectful, honest, and non-judgmental. When conflict arises, couples should also strive to stay present in the conversation and listen actively to the other wife's perspective.

Difficult conversations can be uncomfortable, but they can also be opportunities for growth within a relationship when both parents approach them with openness and respect.

- Choose the right time and place to have the conversation.
- Speak calmly and respectfully.
- Acknowledge the other person's feelings.
- Express your feelings without attacking or blaming the other person.
- Be open to hearing their perspective and feelings.
- Work together to find a solution that is beneficial for both of you.

Setting boundaries with a wife or spouse is essential to parenting a newborn. Establishing clear expectations and limits helps to create a sense of calm and security for the baby. It also helps to prevent disagreements, resentments, and confusion between parents as they adjust to caring for their new family member.

Boundaries provide structure and organization that can make life easier for both parents. Additionally, setting boundaries allows each parent to engage in self-care and practice healthy relationship habits that are vital for the entire family's well-being.

- Establish your feelings and beliefs and be clear and firm about them.
- Think about what is reasonable to expect from the other person.
- Respect the other person's boundaries as well.
- Communicate openly and honestly with each other.
- Talk about any changes in the boundaries that need to be made to keep everything in balance.
- Reassess your boundaries regularly to ensure they are still working for everyone involved.

Difficult conversations can be uncomfortable, but they are necessary to get to the heart of unresolved issues. They provide an opportunity to express feelings and opinions honestly and respectfully and discuss potential solutions or paths forward.

Difficult conversations also help build understanding and trust between parents as they learn how to communicate effectively. A difficult conversation can help resolve disagreements and bring both people closer.

Compromise is essential for any healthy relationship as it helps parents to find common ground and reach a mutually satisfactory conclusion. It involves giving up something to benefit both parties while allowing each wife the freedom to express their needs and wants.

Compromise helps couples create an environment of trust, respect, and understanding which can help them navigate life's challenges together more effectively. It is important to remember that compromise does not mean sacrificing one's desires or values; rather, it means finding a balance between two different perspectives.

Compromising requires communication and both parties being willing to make concessions. Here are some tips for effectively engaging in compromise:

- Listen actively to the other person's point of view.
- Take a step back from the situation and consider how your needs could be met without going against what either person wants.
- Make sure to negotiate fairly, considering both parents' desires.
- Express your feelings openly and honestly but remain respectful during the conversation.
- Be open to solutions that have yet to be initially considered by either party.
- Allow room for flexibility and creativity when finding a mutually agreeable solution.
- Acknowledge each other's efforts in finding a compromise, even if it is still a work in progress.

When Your Wife Blames You During Pregnancy

As a husband, learning how to support his wife with the emotional, mental, and physical changes she experiences during her pregnancy can be daunting. It is important to understand that your wife may feel a range of emotions and needs physical and emotional comfort.

There are practical ways to provide this level of support, including offering words of love and understanding, assisting with errands and housework around the home, exercising together, eating healthy meals, and looking into local support groups if needed.

Nobody knows the true emotions that come along with childbirth like a woman – which means it's important to have patience and understanding during this special time. Even if your wife blames you for something, it can be difficult not to take things personally.

However, it's important to realize that her reactions are based on her hormones and emotions, so take a step back and consider the situation from a distance instead of getting defensive. Remember, she loves you too!

Be a source of emotional and physical support for your wife during her pregnancy. Let your wife express their fears or concerns and provide them with words of love and understanding. Listen attentively to help ease her worries, offer comforting affirmations, and be present with her both in the highs and lows of pregnancy.

Where possible, provide practical ways to manage physical changes such as exercising together, eating healthy meals, massages, and responsible use of medications if needed. Additionally, ask how you can help with errands such as grocery shopping or making appointments so that she feels supported throughout the journey.

Be prepared to face mood swings, attitude changes, and other behaviors that may come up during your wife's pregnancy. It is natural for your wife to face various emotions, so try not to take everything personally or get too defensive.

Listen attentively and try to provide her with words of support and comfort even if she seems unresponsive. Additionally, be mindful of how you respond when your wife asks for help and handle disagreements positively without getting upset or frustrated.

Learning the basics of prenatal care and childbirth is vital to understanding the process and preparing for any decisions that may need to be made throughout the pregnancy. Become familiar with the stages of childbirth and possible complications and understand what tests are done during each trimester.

Additionally, learn about lifestyle changes such as diet, exercise, medications, and other factors that can affect a woman's health during this period. Be sure to voice your questions and concerns during prenatal visits to provide your wife with the best care possible.

Attending doctor visits with your wife during her pregnancy can be a great way to stay informed about the changes in your body and health.

Doing this can help both of you with better peace of mind and ensure that important updates aren't missed between prenatal visits. Being present for checkups can also allow you to ask questions and gain a deeper understanding of what is happening throughout her pregnancy journey.

Throughout the pregnancy journey, it is important to remember that any changes or complications experienced by your wife are not within your control.

Even with the best care, unexpected circumstances can arise during this time. Therefore, it is essential to maintain an atmosphere of understanding and love to provide emotional support and comfort throughout the process.

Being a supportive wife during your pregnancy journey is crucial. Being present for doctor's visits and understanding that any changes or complications are not in your control can help foster an atmosphere of love and support that will last far beyond the duration of the pregnancy.

Join a Support Group

The transition into a new fatherhood is filled with both joy and uncertainty. While it can be an exciting time, it can also be a confusing and overwhelming experience that requires support and guidance.

Having someone to talk to during this transition can provide valuable advice, reassurance, and comfort that are essential to navigating this important stage in life, whether it is a mentor who has already gone through the process or a support group of other fathers who are going through the same journey as you, having someone who understands your unique situation can make all the difference in how you adapt to your new role as a father.

Finding a mentor is a great way for new fathers to gain insight and advice during the transition into fatherhood. When looking for the right mentor, it is important to consider qualities such as trustworthiness, availability, and experience.

Once you have identified the characteristics you are looking for in a mentor, you can look at potential mentors in different settings, such as family members, friends, coworkers, or even online forums.

You can also ask people who already have experience of being fathers or parents to help put you in contact with someone who can provide guidance and wisdom during this process.

Joining a support group of other new fathers can be a great way to share your joys and frustrations during the transition into fatherhood. Not only will you be able to find friends going through the same experience as you, but you will also benefit from having access to resources and information that can help make the process easier.

A support group of new fathers can provide an outlet for important conversations about parenting, give you advice on how to handle common challenges, and even provide an opportunity for fun activities such as game nights or father-son bonding opportunities.

Finding a mentor or joining a support group is an important part of the transition into fatherhood. Not only will these connections provide someone to talk to and advice from those who have been through it before, but they can also help provide much-needed support during this time of adjustment.

A mentor's experience and guidance can help you tackle many common challenges with becoming a father. At the same time, the collective wisdom and camaraderie of being in a support group can give new fathers a sense of community and camaraderie.

A support system is essential for fathers to ensure that both baby and mother are safe before, during and after delivery.

Establishing a network of individuals who can provide emotional, physical, and medical support will help the father navigate any obstacles they may encounter while helping their wife through labor and delivery. The following outlines the steps necessary for establishing a successful support system.

1. Identify individuals who can provide emotional, physical, and medical support during labor and delivery.

2. Establish clear communication channels between the father, healthcare providers, and other individuals in the support system.

3. Delegate responsibilities to different support system members, such as having someone keep track of prenatal appointments and other preparations leading up to delivery.

4. Make sure that everyone involved is aware of any risks or complications that may arise during labor and delivery to have an informed plan in place if needed.

5. Develop systems for staying connected throughout the labor process, such as technology-based solutions or landline phone calls if cell reception is unreliable at the hospital or birthing facility.

6. Utilize resources such as childbirth classes or books regarding what fathers should expect so that they are adequately prepared to assist their wives through labor and delivery.

Baby Shower - Do Not Make Assumptions

New dads often think taking care of the baby shower is someone else's responsibility. But the truth is, the new dad should be aware and prepared for this special occasion.

Baby showers are a time for celebration and an opportunity to bring family and friends together to prepare for the newborn's arrival. New dads must understand their role in ensuring this event goes off without a hitch. We will discuss why it is so important for new dads to know about baby shower planning and preparation and how they can ensure things go smoothly.

Baby showers are a wonderful opportunity for expectant mothers and their families to show their love and support.

Family members, friends, and colleagues will gather to celebrate the new arrival and provide useful items the new parents may need when the baby arrives. It is important for expectant fathers too to understand not only what baby showers are but also how to prepare them.

New dads should take some time to be proactive in helping with ideas for themes, decorations, invitations, gifts, and other preparations related to the baby shower. By being involved in preparing for this special event, they can create an enjoyable experience that everyone involved can cherish.

- So this doesn't mean it's your responsibility, but don't be oblivious.
- Research and create a list of potential venues to host the baby shower.
- Make sure to include a budget when planning the baby shower.
- Put together an invitation list, decide who's invited, and begin sending out invitations.
- Assemble any decorations and favors in advance of the event.
- Have a backup plan if something unexpected happens close to the date of the event.
- Create that baby registry and show some enthusiasm as your wife goes shopping. I had to learn this lesson the hard way.

A baby shower is a time for celebration, love, and anticipation for the newborn. New dads have an important role in making sure that this special event is one that everyone involved can cherish.

They should take the time to be proactive in helping with ideas and preparations for the baby shower. By understanding what is expected of them, new dads can help create a truly memorable experience for everyone involved.

Take Time Out for Yourself

Being a new parent can be overwhelming, but taking time for yourself is important to be a responsible father.

By giving yourself some space from everyday parenting responsibilities and allowing yourself to recharge, you will return to your child or children with a refreshed and more positive outlook. So remember, dads: take some time for yourself now and then! You'll be surprised how it can improve your connection with your little ones.

Taking time for yourself is a beneficial practice for both parents. For new dads, it allows them to step away from the everyday duties of parenting and return reenergized and better equipped to handle their responsibilities.

For the mom, it's an opportunity to take a break from caring for the baby and focus on herself or activities she enjoys. Having time to recharge can give her the energy to provide the best care for her little one when her dad returns. Remember, mamas and papas, taking time out for yourself is key to caring for your child!

Most Common Mistakes

First-time fathers face a multitude of challenges during the pregnancy period. It is important to understand and recognize these common mistakes to better prepare themselves for any surprises that may come up.

Some of the most common mistakes that first-time dads make during pregnancy include failing to be emotionally supportive, not being actively involved in doctor appointments and childbirth classes, not taking responsibility for their health and well-being, not preparing financially for the birth, and not researching about the process of labor and delivery.

By recognizing these potential pitfalls, first-time dads can take proactive steps to avoid making them.

Being involved in planning your baby's birth is crucial for first-time dads. By getting informed about the labor, delivery, and post-birth proceedings, fathers can ensure that everything goes as smoothly as possible.

This can involve attending doctor appointments or childbirth classes with the mother, researching options available at the hospital, and understanding neonatal procedures. Additionally, talking to other parents can provide helpful insights on what to expect during childbirth.

It is important to understand that being active in your baby's birth will benefit you and your wife and give you peace of mind leading up to one of life's greatest moments.

Throughout the pregnancy journey, it is important to recognize and acknowledge your wife's emotions. As partners, both of you need to take time to talk to each other openly and honestly about any questions, concerns, or worries that come up.

One wife may feel more overwhelmed than the other, and this can help ease some of the strain the process can cause. Fathers should also understand their emotions throughout the experience and not be afraid to let their wife know how they feel.

Taking time to talk with each other can ensure stronger communication leading up to the birthday and beyond.

Being prepared for birth is essential for fathers. It is important to plan for the time by gathering all necessary items like diapers, onesies, blankets, and hats. Fathers should consider packing a few essentials in a bag to take with them on the big day — such as snacks, water, or an extra change of clothes in case of emergencies.

Having your vehicle serviced before the due date and ensuring you have enough gas in your tank and a valid driver's license can be helpful. Allowing yourself ample time to get ready will also help reduce stress levels when dealing with spontaneous labor or delivery circumstances.

When expecting, it is important to start making plans for childcare after the baby arrives.

Fathers should begin researching their options and exploring daycare facilities and nanny services that would fit their family's needs. It can also be helpful to seek help from grandparents or other family members who may live nearby.

Making plans is essential for fathers to have peace of mind knowing that their little ones will be taken care of after birth.

Fathers should also consider their financial capabilities when making childcare arrangements. They may need to look into filing for parental leave or taking unpaid days off work to care for their new little one. It is wise to start budgeting ahead, adding childcare costs and other necessary expenses associated with a baby's birth.

Additionally, parents should look into the various government programs that offer financial assistance regarding childcare. Making sure you have the financial means to provide for your baby will help ensure a smooth transition from pregnancy to parenthood.

Here are some action items fathers should consider when making plans for childcare after the baby is born:

- Explore getting help from grandparents or other family members who may live nearby
- File for parental leave or take unpaid days off work to care for their little one
- Budget ahead of time and add in childcare costs and any other necessary expenses associated with a baby's birth
- Look into government programs that offer financial assistance for childcare.

Doing the necessary research ahead of time will give fathers peace of mind knowing they have taken all possible steps to provide the best care for their little one.

Be Part of the Planning

During one of the most exciting and life-changing times for parents, expectant fathers have a unique role in planning for their newborns.

To ensure that a baby is provided with the best possible care, fathers need to research ahead of time to become knowledgeable about options for childcare and other important decisions.

Neglecting to be part of the planning process can lead to several issues and complications during and after childbirth. Fathers should ensure they are adequately prepared and educated in providing the best care for their infants.

Fathers should feel empowered to partake in the planning process, as they have a right to be involved in decisions about their children.

They understand that fathers have an important role to play by doing the necessary research to become informed about all options for childcare, filing for parental leave or unpaid days off, budgeting appropriately, and exploring government programs that can provide financial assistance with childcare costs.

Doing this early on will help fathers feel prepared to take on their new responsibilities confidently.

Fathers need to understand that they have an important role in their children's lives and that it's just as important for them to be involved in the planning process as it is for mothers.

Early learning about childcare costs and options, filing for parental leave or unpaid days off, budgeting appropriately, and exploring government programs that can provide financial assistance will help fathers provide the best care possible for their newborns.

Additionally, understanding how to create a safe and secure environment at home should also be a priority during this stage.

Ultimately, by taking all these steps into account, fathers can participate meaningfully in one of life's most special times with confidence.

While planning for the arrival of a new baby is exciting, it's important to understand that preparing for childbirth can be a stressful experience. Considering seeking professional medical advice from certified professionals should be an early priority on the to-do list.

Certified midwives, doulas, and other healthcare practitioners can provide invaluable guidance on labor and delivery techniques, postpartum care, managing breast or bottle feeding, sleeping strategies for infants, and more.

Taking advantage of their expertise can help ensure that fathers are well-prepared when it comes time to welcome their newborns into the world.

Both parents must remain open and communicative throughout the pregnancy. Doing so will create a sense of understanding, collaboration, and trust between them, helping to strengthen the bond before the baby's arrival. Additionally, parents must discuss their feelings and expectations regarding parenting responsibilities.

Having these conversations early can help set realistic expectations and avoid potential disagreements in the future. Fathers should be especially mindful of expressing discomfort or anxiety about welcoming a new baby. This can help create an emotionally safe environment for both parents before the baby arrives.

- Have open, honest conversations with your wife throughout the pregnancy to ensure understanding and collaboration.
- Discuss expectations of parenting responsibilities early on to set realistic expectations.
- Fathers should be mindful of expressing anxieties about welcoming a new baby, as this can help create an emotionally safe environment.
- Consider seeking professional medical advice and guidance from certified midwives, doulas, and healthcare professionals who can provide invaluable information regarding labor and delivery techniques, postpartum care, breast or bottle feeding methods, sleeping strategies for infants, and more.

It's important to think ahead and consider potential scenarios of concern during the pregnancy, which could require medical or emotional support.

This could include discussions about the possibility of a high-risk pregnancy, what would happen if medical interventions became necessary, or how to manage stress during this time. It is also important to create a safety plan with your wife or doctor in case any unexpected situations arise during the pregnancy.

A safety plan is a plan of action that can be taken in anticipation or response to a potential high-risk scenario during the pregnancy. This could include deciding when and where to seek medical attention, coping strategies for stress, and how the wife, family members, or doctors can best provide support.

It's important to create a tailored safety plan with your doctor to ensure you receive the best possible care and support for yourself and your baby.

- Create an open dialogue with your wife to discuss expectations, anxieties, and lifestyle changes.
- Seek professional medical advice from certified midwives, doulas, and healthcare professionals.
- Draft a tailored safety plan with your doctor to anticipate potential high-risk scenarios.
- Discuss coping strategies if stress becomes intense.
- Ask family members or doctors how they may be able to provide support.

An open dialogue with your wife will help set realistic expectations for the coming months, ensuring that both parties feel comfortable and supported. It is also important to discuss any anxieties related to the pregnancy and financial, emotional, and lifestyle changes that may occur.

Professional medical advice should be sought from certified midwives, doulas, and healthcare professionals who can provide invaluable information regarding labor and delivery techniques, postpartum care, breast- or bottle-feeding methods, sleeping strategies for infants, potential high-risk scenarios that could require medical support or emotional guidance.

Several coping strategies can help manage stress and stay grounded, including mindfulness and deep breathing exercises, carving out time for yourself, pursuing counseling or therapy sessions, making lifestyle changes like healthy eating habits and regular sleep, and engaging in relaxing activities like reading or listening to music.

They are creating a reliable network of family members and friends who can provide emotional guidance and assistance if needed is also crucial. With the right preparation and support, expecting parents can be better equipped to handle the anxieties that come with parenthood.

- You are carving out time for yourself and engaging in relaxing activities

that you enjoy, such as reading or listening to music.
- Practicing mindfulness and deep breathing exercises to stay grounded.
- Creating a strong support system with family members and friends who can provide emotional guidance and assistance.
- Pursuing counseling or therapy sessions with a licensed therapist if necessary.
- Making lifestyle changes, such as adequate sleep, healthy eating habits, light exercise, and regular social interactions.

Preparing for labor and delivery, postpartum care, breastfeeding or bottle-feeding methods, and sleeping strategies for infants are important steps that parents should take before the birth of their baby. Researching such topics can provide knowledge and insight that can reduce stress surrounding parenthood in the future.

This may include attending childbirth classes with one's wife or other family members, reading books about parenting, taking tours at a hospital or birth center, and gathering information. Access to these resources can help give new parents the confidence to manage any obstacles they may face during pregnancy and after.

Additionally, they should familiarize themselves with applicable laws and regulations that could impact new parents. This could include policies surrounding parental leave, workplace rules surrounding caring for a newborn, and other relevant laws that may affect their job or family life after the birth of their child.

Knowing these policies beforehand can help ensure that dads know their rights and responsibilities as new parents.

Doing all this can help ensure dads feel informed and prepared to care for their newborns properly.

Go to the OBGYN Appointment

As an expectant father, you have an important role in your baby's health and development. Attending regular OBGYN appointments is essential for any parent-to-be, as it provides a wealth of information about the mother's health and the unborn baby's growth.

You can also ask questions, receive advice from experienced practitioners, and get support when necessary. Remember that these visits are not just for moms but for dads too! Don't miss out on an OBGYN appointment – even if you're the dad!

Prenatal care is an important part of a woman's pregnancy journey.

During routine OBGYN appointments, your wife can talk with a doctor or midwife about her physical and emotional health. At each visit, the healthcare team will measure your wife's uterus size and weight gain, check vital signs such as blood pressure, and ask questions about lifestyle habits like stress levels, diet, and activity level.

Depending on your wife's pregnancy stage, other tests may include urine testing for infection or gestational diabetes, ultrasound scans to check the baby's position and movements, and additional prenatal screenings for conditions like Down Syndrome or other chromosomal abnormalities.

Your wife will also be able to ask any questions she might have about her pregnancy – from advice on morning sickness or leg cramps to labor preparation and delivery options.

With regular visits throughout your wife's pregnancy, you can both ensure that she is taking care of herself and getting ready for the arrival of your baby!

As a dad-to-be, it's important to stay as informed and involved in your wife's prenatal care as possible. Not only will this help provide her with emotional support, but it is also an opportunity for you to discuss any concerns or questions you may have.

Be sure to attend checkup appointments with your wife whenever you can and familiarize yourself with the common tests and treatments associated with pregnancy.

Talk to the doctor or midwife about any specific risks associated with your wife's pregnancy, including genetic testing and other screenings if necessary.

Encourage your wife to make healthy lifestyle choices during her pregnancy – drink plenty of fluids, get adequate rest (but do not overdo it!), and try regular exercise throughout the day. Above all, lend a listening ear when she needs it most!

During these visits, the doctor or midwife will have plenty of helpful information on nutrition, lifestyle habits, and general safety protocols. It's also a good time to ask questions about the labor and delivery process or what help you need during your wife's recovery.

Additionally, OBGYN practitioners can advise about breastfeeding, child-care options, and any other family planning matters you may consider. Don't hesitate to take advantage of these invaluable resources!

As a new dad, getting all the information you can from your wife's OBGYN is important. Questions to ask might include:

- What kind of tests are recommended during pregnancy?
- Are there any potential risks associated with my wife's current condition?
- How long should her postpartum recovery period be?
- What lifestyle modifications can we make to facilitate a healthy birth and recovery?
- Are there any resources or services available for new parents in our community?

Other good questions to ask the OBGYN include:

- What kind of prenatal vitamins should my wife be taking?
- Should there be any activities or habits we should avoid during pregnancy?
- What exercises or stretches can help keep her body fit for labor and delivery?
- Are there any special dietary requirements that need to be considered during pregnancy?

· What symptoms should she watch out for before going into labor?

HIPAA (the Health Insurance Portability and Accountability Act) is a law that protects patients' privacy by preventing their medical information from being shared without explicit permission. This means that even though you are the father, your wife's OBGYN cannot discuss her health with you without her permission or signing a waiver.

It also applies to other members of her healthcare team, such as nurses and midwives. Protecting your wife's right to privacy is important, so make sure she makes an informed decision before signing any waivers.

It can be incredibly frustrating for new dads when they cannot get answers to their most pressing questions because of HIPAA laws. This can often lead to a sense of helplessness and confusion, especially when ensuring the health of both mother and baby is taken care of.

Furthermore, it can be difficult for the father to feel connected with the pregnancy if he's unable to be involved in decision-making due to HIPAA laws.

Yes, dads should know that their wives' OBGYN is bound by HIPAA laws to protect their patients' privacy.

This means that, even if the father is present during the appointment, the doctor cannot discuss his wife's medical information with him unless she provides explicit permission. Furthermore, he should ensure that he and his wife are informed about any waivers that need to be signed before any medical information can be shared with him.

Yes, a doctor can have private conversations with the father of an unborn baby if the mother has given explicit permission to discuss her medical information. However, HIPAA laws still apply, and the doctor cannot share any information without the mother's consent.

The doctor can guide prenatal care, nutrition, and other general health matters, but anything specific to the mother must be discussed privately with her before being shared with the father.

Attending an appointment together solidifies the bond between parent and child and ensures that both parents know any decisions or plans surrounding their unborn baby. This is especially important during pregnancy, as decisions made by the mother can have a lasting impact on the health and well-being of the baby and the mother.

By attending these appointments with his wife, a father can show his love and support for her and help ensure that all decisions regarding their unborn baby will be those he is comfortable with.

Attending regular OBGYN appointments with your wife allows you to receive support from the practitioner and other family members.

From understanding diagnoses and managing side effects to finding solutions to common issues during pregnancy, having a supportive wife along for the ride can make all the difference in making informed decisions throughout this important journey.

Not only can attending these visits provide dads with the information they need, but it also serves as an invaluable source of strength and reassurance as they embark on this life-changing experience.

Attending OBGYN appointments with your wife provides many other benefits for new dads. One of the most important is learning to provide support when making decisions about delivery methods and childbirth options.

Additionally, these visits allow new dads to become more familiar with their baby's development and gain insight into their role as a father, which can be immensely beneficial during this exciting time. Finally, attending OBGYN appointments can ensure that both parents do everything they can to ensure a healthy pregnancy and childbirth.

Ignoring Emotional Requirements

It is easy to feel overwhelmed by a newborn baby, especially regarding meeting their physical needs. But it is just as important – if not more – to remember to nourish and nurture their emotional requirements.

As parents, taking the time and energy to ensure your baby has the best possible start in life emotionally as well as physically is one of the most rewarding challenges you may ever face.

Pregnancy can be an exciting and thrilling time for expecting parents. Although physical changes are expected during this time, paying attention to your wife's emotional needs is equally important.

A supportive environment for your wife during this transition can help her feel valued, appreciated, and secure. Understanding the emotional support she requires can help your family enjoy a positive pregnancy experience and bond with your new arrival.

It can be difficult for new dads to adjust and cope with their wife's emotional needs during pregnancy.

One of the best things a first-time dad can do is to make sure they are available to talk about and address their wife's feelings, worries, and concerns. Allowing your wife to open up and share her thoughts will create an environment where she feels comfortable and secure enough to express herself.

With supportive communication, it is possible to build a strong foundation for both of you as parents before the baby arrives. Another way for new dads to show support during pregnancy is by making small gestures that let their wives know she is cared for.

A simple back rub or spending time together over dinner can go a long way in showing her she matters and demonstrating how much you appreciate her throughout this special journey together.

As a new dad, it's important to make yourself available to your wife and listen to her feelings and concerns throughout her pregnancy. Showing you care by being an open and active participant in conversations can go a long way in building trust between you both as partners and as parents.

It is important to remember that each pregnancy can be different, so staying informed and understanding her feelings is key in providing support during this special time.

Remember that your wife's emotional well-being is just as important as the physical aspects of having a baby, so ensure you're providing the necessary care and attention during this magical period for both of you.

During pregnancy, fathers-to-be need to remain open-minded and flexible. Showing patience, empathy, and understanding will go a long way in supporting your wife as different needs arise.

To be better prepared, reading up on what to expect during each trimester — and the entire pregnancy journey — can help you understand the changes that might occur along the way. Staying educated throughout this time can help you become a positive and supportive wife.

Patience is an important quality to have as a supportive wife during pregnancy. Listening attentively and understanding can help you show patience and engage in meaningful dialogue with your wife.

Taking time to reflect on your and your wife's emotions can help you remain patient and be there for them throughout the pregnancy. Additionally, offering support without pressuring or pushing them can demonstrate patience in times of need.

Empathy is essential in showing support during pregnancy. Taking time to understand the needs and emotions of your wife — without making judgments — can be beneficial in demonstrating empathy.

You can also help provide emotional relief by listening and validating their feelings, understanding where they're coming from, and offering comfort when necessary. Simple acts such as giving a hug or helping with household tasks can show your wife that you're there for them.

Men often struggle with empathy and understanding during pregnancy due to their emotions, views, and societal and cultural norms. Their understanding of the process can be limited, and they may have difficulty relating to or recognizing their wife's feelings.

However, by listening and understanding, they can develop a deeper appreciation for what their wife is going through—this helps create an empathetic environment that allows them to demonstrate support without judgment.

Empathy is not something you are born with or have from the beginning, but it is a skill that can be developed and improved over time through mindful and meaningful interactions.

Listening to your wife's needs and emotions with an open mind and heart will help to build empathy. Also, asking questions to gain more insight into how they feel can show your wife that you care about what they're going through. With dedication and effort, you can cultivate an empathetic environment that is beneficial for everyone involved.

A new dad can develop empathy for his wife by observing her experiences, understanding her emotions and needs, and being mindful of how his reactions may impact her.

Taking the time to listen to her and ask questions to clarify what she is going through can help create an empathetic bond that will benefit both individuals. Also, trying to recognize the physical and emotional changes occurring during pregnancy can help develop empathy.

Here are five steps to help a new dad develop empathy for his wife:

- Take the time to listen. Listen to your wife's concerns and worries, understand her emotions, and needs, and ask questions if necessary.
- Validate her experiences. Acknowledge the physical and emotional changes occurring during pregnancy and any fears or anxieties your wife may have about it.
- Respect her feelings. Show respect for her feelings, even if you do not agree with them, by putting yourself in her shoes and trying to see things from her perspective.
- Offer practical support. Offer practical assistance, such as helping with household chores, running errands, or providing emotional support.
- Be available for each other. Try to spend quality time together regularly and use this time to reconnect with each other through meaningful conversations or activities that both of you enjoy doing together.

Baby Moons

As a new dad, it is important to be understanding and compassionate toward your wife's needs, even if they do not align with your own.

Denying her request for a break or vacation during tough times can damage your attempt to develop empathy, as it could make her feel unsupported and unheard. Instead of denying her request, try offering alternative solutions that both of you can agree on.

A baby moon is a special trip couples take before having their first child. The purpose of the trip is to take some time out for themselves and reconnect with each other before the challenges of parenthood start to set in.

This can be a wonderful way for couples to relax, unwind and create lasting memories together before the arrival of their new baby.

It is especially important to plan a baby moon before the third trimester, as it may be more challenging to travel while pregnant. When planning your baby moon, investigate any restrictions your destination may have regarding pregnancy.

Furthermore, you will want to prioritize comfort and safety when selecting your mode of transportation and accommodation.

It is safe for pregnant women to fly before 36 weeks (about 8 and a half months) of pregnancy but speaking with a healthcare provider first is advised. During the flight, buckling up and drinking plenty of fluids is important, as well as avoiding gassy foods.

After 36 weeks (about 8 and a half months), some airlines may not allow pregnant passengers or require a letter from the health care provider specifying the length of pregnancy. Additionally, pregnant people should be aware that air travel can increase the risk of blood clots in the legs and radiation exposure.

Health Effects of Air Travel

Here are some other potential health effects of air travel and pregnancy:

- Difficulty breathing, dizziness, headaches, and even depression due to altitude and cabin pressure changes.
- It is swelling in the feet, legs, and hands from sitting for extended periods.
- Get up and move around periodically throughout the flight.
- Wear compression stockings or socks to help reduce swelling.
- Try to elevate your legs as much as possible.
- Drink plenty of water to avoid dehydration.
- Uncomfortable seating can make getting a good rest during the flight

difficult.

- Air travel can raise the risk of blood clots in the legs, a condition called venous thrombosis, which is higher for pregnant people.
- Take walks up and down the aisle every hour during the flight, or flex and extend your ankles from time to time if you must remain seated. Wear compression stockings to help with blood circulation during a long flight.

New dads are often overwhelmed with caring for a newborn, and it can be difficult to adjust to the demands of it. But for fathers, refusing to make necessary lifestyle adjustments to accommodate their wife's needs better is one of the biggest mistakes they will ever make.

These adjustments include getting more sleep, eating better meals, and practicing regular self-care. Making these choices early on will ensure that both parents can provide adequate support for their new baby while still having enough energy left over for each other.

Despite being one of the most emotional times in a woman's life, pregnancy can often be a lonely experience for a new mother-to-be.

Coupled with dramatic physical and hormonal changes, fathers need to acknowledge, understand, and address their wife's emotional needs during this time.

Neglecting to do so can lead to feelings of loneliness, increased stress, and even depression. You should encourage your wife to express their feelings and find ways to provide comfort and reassurance during this delicate time.

Regular date nights away from the baby benefit the couple and promote happy memories during pregnancy that they will cherish later.

Pregnancy can be a roller coaster of emotions for any woman. The range of feelings she will experience can be overwhelming, from fear and confusion to joy and excitement.

Exhaustion, caused by the sudden hormone increase, is also quite common throughout pregnancy. Anxiety is another emotion that many pregnant women struggle with due to all the unknowns associated with welcoming a new baby into their lives.

These feelings must be addressed and supported so that the mother-to-be's mental and physical health remains strong during this special time. Soon-to-be dads must practice understanding and patience as they provide emotional support during their pregnancy.

· Identify and acknowledge your wife's emotional needs during pregnancy.
· Provide comfort and reassurance whenever possible.
· Find ways to make her feel special, such as regular date nights.
· Encourage her to express her feelings without judgment.
· Show understanding and patience when she experiences anxiety or fear.
· Regularly reminds her of the joys of welcoming a new baby into their lives.

Supporting your wife during pregnancy is essential for her mental and physical health. Here are some strategies to help you do this:

· Recognize the range of emotions she may be experiencing, such as fear, exhaustion, joy, and anxiety.
· Provide comfort and reassurance by listening to her concerns and offering encouragement.
· Surprise her with gestures to make her feel special, such as thoughtful gifts or a romantic dinner date.
· Allow for open communication so that she can express her feelings without judgment.
· Show understanding and patience when she experiences panic or worry.
· Tell her how amazing it will be when their baby arrives.

It's important to remember that pregnancy is a roller coaster of emotions for any woman. From fear and confusion to joy and excitement, it can be an overwhelming experience.

This makes it essential for soon-to-be dads to provide emotional support during this special time through understanding, patience, comfort, reassurance, and little gestures of love.

By acknowledging your wife's needs throughout her pregnancy journey, you'll help ensure her mental and physical health remain strong as she awaits the arrival of your new bundle of joy!

What is a Push Gift?

Hey first-time dads, have you heard of a push gift? A push gift is a present that some dads give to their wives after they give birth.

It's a way of saying thanks for all her hard work bringing your child into the world. Some people think push gifts are a great idea, and if you're thinking about getting one for your wife, read on to find out more.

A push gift is a great way to show your wife how much you care, especially after she goes through childbirth! Instead of showering her with standard congratulatory gifts, go the extra mile and surprise her with something special that she'll cherish forever - whether it's a piece of jewelry or spa treatments.

Let her know just how much you appreciate all she did to bring this miracle into your life.

Being a parent is no easy feat; your wife experienced many changes during pregnancy and labor. Showing your appreciation for all she went through is a great way to let her know how much you care.

From sore feet, bigger jeans, and sleepless nights - you both have come out of this journey with an amazing new addition to your family!

Make sure you thank her properly - offer her a foot massage, bring home dinner so she does not have to cook, or send a heartfelt card. Anything that can make her feel appreciated will go a long way in showing just how much you truly value all of her hard work!

When gifting your mom something special, the only limit is your creativity. It doesn't have to be expensive either - anything you put a lot of thought into will always make her feel special. You can bake her favorite dessert or make her something with two hands.

Or perhaps she's a fan of precious jewelry - modern or antique, any trinket that you know she'll love and treasure for a long time will surely give her joy.

Or treat her to a spa day so she can have some peace and relaxation from the comfort of her home – and maybe even get some well-deserved me-time! No matter what it is, remember that the gesture itself holds more value than whatever it is you're gifting.

When it comes to giving a push gift, you want to put some thought into it. This isn't just any type of gift - it celebrates the incredible accomplishment of bringing a baby into the world! Choose something that has a special meaning and will make your wife feel appreciated.

She will be touched by your thoughtfulness when you present her with the perfect push gift - something she will cherish for years. Whether it is a piece of jewelry, a special memento, or anything else you think she'll love, make sure to choose wisely.

Not Being Ready for Birth

No matter how much you plan and prepare, there is no way to guarantee that you will be ready for the day your baby arrives. Even if you are ready, there is always a chance that something unexpected could happen and change the course of events.

The days leading up to delivery can be incredibly stressful – full of emotions and anticipation.

Take care of yourself during this time and have an open dialogue with your doctor or midwife about any questions or concerns you may have. Have a plan in place so that you can be aware of what will happen in the event of any potential complications.

Ask for tips from other parents who have gone through labor before, and make sure you know where all the important medical care is located near your home – just in case.

Try to relax and enjoy the experience no matter what happens - it will never come again!

Before giving birth, it is important to plan and ensure everything is in place. Ensure you have all the necessary resources available during labor, such as a birthing plan, supplies, home births, equipment, and documentaries.

Ensure your home is adequately prepared – a well-stocked pantry, washed bedding, and prepared nursery – so that you are not scrambling when the time comes. It may also be helpful to consider alternative options or arrangements for delivery or postpartum care if something unexpected happens.

Developing a childbirth strategy is a terrific way to help ensure your and your baby's health and safety.

Working with an experienced obstetrician or midwife is key to helping decide on the best birth method, pain management techniques, safety precautions, and other topics related to labor.

It's essential to have regular check-ups during pregnancy to monitor the progress of your baby's development and discuss any worries or concerns regarding delivery.

Discuss any potential risks associated with labor and delivery that could affect the mother or baby's safety. Having a plan in place will give you peace of mind knowing that everything possible has been done before the delivery day. Remember to trust yourself and your body – you can bring forth life!

Emotional Requirements - Postpartum

As you are supporting your wife through this transition, you must consider her emotional needs during the postpartum period.

Please don't dismiss the importance of meeting your wife's emotional requirements, as this can seriously affect her mental and physical health. Being attuned to her needs and providing comfort, understanding, and reassurance will help her navigate this new journey more confidently.

By taking these essential steps, you can ensure that your wife and baby receive the best care throughout pregnancy and beyond.

Neglecting your wife's emotional needs after pregnancy can lead to profound consequences, so it is important to be attentive and supportive of her during this postpartum period.

It is important to give your wife the emotional support she needs after pregnancy for assorted reasons. Primarily, it helps her adjust to the physical and emotional changes that come with childbirth. Additionally, it can help alleviate feelings of depression or stress that may arise during this challenging period.

Furthermore, providing your wife with emotional comfort post-birth can help strengthen your relationship and ensure a healthy bond between you. Lastly, it can benefit both her and the baby's happiness as she will be better equipped to handle any challenges along their parenting journey.

Neglecting your postpartum wife's emotional needs can lead to various detrimental consequences. For instance, she may be prone to isolation and loneliness due to your lack of reassurance and comfort.

This could lead to signs of depression or anxiety due to the stress of caring for her newborn without emotional support. In extreme cases, neglecting her emotional needs postpartum can even result in physical complications such as fatigue or high blood pressure due to her inability to cope with the strain.

To avoid such outcomes, you must pay attention to and act upon your wife's emotional needs in the postpartum period.

Here is an action plan to support your wife emotionally during postpartum:

- Spend quality time with her every day. Talk, listen, and empathize with her struggles.
- Let her take breaks from the baby when needed.
- Cook meals for her and help out with chores around the house;
- Show physical affection, such as giving hugs and holding hands.
- Offer words of encouragement when she's feeling overwhelmed or discouraged;
- Reach out to extended family members or friends for additional assistance if available;
- Take care of yourself by eating healthy meals and getting enough sleep so that you can be refreshed for your wife's needs;
- Identify any underlying mental health issues and seek professional help if needed;
- Connect with other couples in similar situations who can offer perspec-

tives and advice on better handling postpartum challenges.

Postpartum can be an emotional roller coaster for new mothers, with many feelings that can sometimes overwhelm them. Common emotions experienced during this period include:

- Joy: Most women feel tremendous joy when they become mothers and are excited to start this new chapter.
- Anxiety: New moms often worry about being able to provide the best care for their babies and feel anxious about making mistakes.
- Sadness: Postpartum depression is very common after giving birth, and many women experience deep sadness or bouts of crying due to hormonal changes.
- Loneliness: Many new mothers feel isolated from friends and family who may not understand what they're going through.
- Exhaustion: Caring for a newborn can be physically and mentally exhausting, so sometimes it's normal to feel fatigued and overwhelmed.

Here are some strategies for supporting and meeting your wife's emotional requirements after birth:

- Initiate conversation and take the time to listen to her needs, feelings, and worries.
- Offer physical affection, such as giving hugs and holding hands;
- Express appreciation for what she's doing with words of encouragement.
- Give her space when needed and allow her to take naps or breaks from the baby without judgment.
- Invite close family members or friends over who can offer additional support;
- Share in some of the responsibilities, so she can have more time to rest and recoup;
- Establish a postpartum care plan with your spouse so that you both understand what is expected following childbirth;

- Connecting with other couples in similar situations can provide insight into managing postpartum struggles more effectively.

Ignoring the emotional requirements of a new mother can have profound consequences. Without adequate support, new mothers may suffer from depression and anxiety, be more prone to sickness, and struggle with parenting their newborns.

Emotional turmoil can also lead to relationship issues between parents and difficulty trusting that they can care for their infant. To avoid these outcomes, it's important to take mothers' emotional needs seriously by offering compassion, understanding, and a listening ear during this often-challenging period in their lives.

Additionally, seek out professional help if needed. It is not a sign of weakness to ask for assistance, and many resources are available to new mothers who need extra support. Postpartum care plans can include visits with licensed therapists and counselors and consultations with doulas and certified postpartum educators.

Motherhood can be incredibly rewarding with an approach that values physical and emotional well-being.

With the right support, new mothers can feel confident and capable as they embark on this incredible adventure.

By working together to meet emotional needs and providing encouragement, couples can create a positive postpartum experience and foster a strong, lasting connection. With understanding and care, you can help your wife enjoy the joys of motherhood while taking steps to ensure her well-being.

Creating a Birth Plan

It's exciting when a couple finds out what they expect! As a first-time dad, you will naturally want to do everything you can to support your wife during the birthing process and ensure a healthy delivery. A birth plan can just be a couple of pages, more like a checklist of wishes if you were to have the perfect delivery.

But let's face it. Murphey's law will rear its ugly head when you least expect it. Anything can occur during labor and delivery. Caution: Remain flexible here. Don't be so set on the birth plan that it interferes with the medical professionals who are there to ensure the safety of baby and mom.

One of the best ways to do this is to be involved in crafting a birth plan. Both parents need a say in such an important moment, so don't leave it all up to mom – get involved! You can take on the role of advocate, helping her make informed decisions while understanding the available options.

A solid birth plan will give you peace of mind and help everyone feel more secure during labor and delivery.

It's important to have a birth plan before your baby's arrival, so you are both prepared and informed.

A plan ensures that the delivery is as safe, comfortable, and successful as possible.

By having a birth plan, you can make sure that all of your preferences are taken into account, such as the type of delivery, pain management techniques for labor and delivery, the supplies and equipment needed for the birth, who will be present in the delivery room with you, and postpartum care essentials.

A birth plan also helps to ensure that you both remain on the same page during the birthing process. Having a clear understanding of what to expect can help reduce stress or potential disagreements while your wife is in labor.

It is important to include in the birth plan anyone present in the delivery room during labor and delivery.

This could include family, friends, medical professionals such as doctors or midwives, and other care providers like doulas or lactation consultants. Additionally, any postpartum care essentials should be included in the plan.

These could include infant care supplies and equipment, home health visits from a pediatrician, or plans for physical or mental recovery after delivery. Talk through these details with your wife to ensure you are both on the same page and consider your wishes for postpartum care.

Other considerations for a birth plan include preferences for managing pain during labor and delivery. Consider the types of interventions you would like to have or avoid, as well as any holistic methods for dealing with pain that you would like to try.

Also, discuss with your wife if there are any religious or cultural practices related to childbirth you want to implement.

Finally, think about how you want to welcome your baby after birth. This could include who will cut the umbilical cord, what type of first bath the baby will receive, or other things like cameras in the delivery room or skin-to-skin contact.

Consider feeding options after birth. This could include breastfeeding, bottle-feeding, or both. If you choose to breastfeed, consider when you will introduce bottles or pacifiers. Also, discuss what formula you may want to use if you decide not to breastfeed.

If a person other than the mother will be feeding the baby at any time, make sure to discuss with your wife who is responsible for preparing bottles and how often they should be given.

Furthermore, many different baby accessories, like swaddles and carriers, can help make life easier - so research these items before putting your birth plan together.

Skin-to-skin contact is an especially important part of the birth plan. It involves holding your baby closely against your skin when they are first born and can be done by either parent.

This contact helps establish a strong bond between parent and child and promotes early breastfeeding success. Many hospitals even have certain policies that enable mothers to hold their babies for the first hour after birth, even if there are complications during delivery.

Keeping a baby skin-to-skin can also reduce stress levels, regulate body temperature, and help them transition to life outside the womb.

Skin-to-skin contact between a mother and her baby is an important part of the birthing process. It fosters an emotional bond between the two and can also reduce stress levels in both wife and child, aiding in the baby's transition into life outside the womb.

Additionally, this type of contact encourages successful breastfeeding. It helps to establish a sense of familiarity for your wife or wife, who may otherwise feel overwhelmed by their new role as a parent.

Keeping baby skin-to-skin with mom immediately after birth can be incredibly beneficial for both mother and baby.

Skin-to-skin contact between the new father and his baby is also beneficial.

Studies have shown that this contact strengthens the emotional bond between parent and child and reduces paternal stress levels. It helps to regulate hormone levels in both the father and baby, improving emotional regulation overall.

Furthermore, skin-to-skin contact with dad encourages breastfeeding success and allows for parental bonding time right away. Making sure a new dad is comfortable with his role during skin-to-skin contact ahead of time can help ease any anxiety he may have about being involved in the birthing process.

At Home Birth

Home births are becoming increasingly popular among parents who want a more intimate and controlled experience with their newborns. Home births allow mothers and their husbands to create a safe, comfortable environment while still being attended by experienced caregivers such as midwives or doulas.

During home births, birth plans can be followed more closely, and the mother has access to resources that may not be available in a hospital setting, like comfort measures such as water immersion or vibration therapy.

Home births also provide the benefit of no time limits on labor, allowing the mother and birthing team to move at her own pace throughout the process. Lastly, home births are cost-effective and often covered by insurance, depending on your plan.

By considering all these factors, parents can make an informed decision about where they want to give birth for the best possible outcome for themselves and their baby.

When considering an at-home birth, it is important to keep several factors in mind:

- It is essential to ensure that you have access to a qualified midwife or doula since they will guide you through the labor and delivery process. It is also important to ensure that the space is comfortable and safe for the mother and baby.
- It is beneficial to have a support system at home or virtually so that you can be surrounded by people who care about your well-being during this special time.
- Research home birth options in your area, as some states may restrict what kind of services can be provided outside of a hospital setting.

By considering all these considerations, parents can make informed decisions about their birth plan and find what works best for them.

Hospital births provide the benefit of being in a location staffed with experienced doctors and nurses trained to handle any unexpected developments during labor and delivery.

Many hospitals offer pain management solutions like epidurals which can make the birthing process more comfortable for those giving birth.

In addition, many hospitals also have an array of resources that may not be available in other settings, like electronic fetal monitoring, to ensure the baby's health and access to medical interventions in the case of complications.

Hospital births also often include more scheduling flexibility since they are typically open at all hours, unlike home births which may require more preparation and planning. Finally, there is often a sense of security knowing that medical professionals surround you should something unexpected occur during your labor and delivery.

It's important to consider your family's needs and preferences when deciding between a home birth or a hospital birth. If you have any underlying medical conditions or a history of medical complications in your family, it may be safer to choose the hospital setting.

Having access to the necessary resources and support can make the at-home birth more comfortable and safer. The best birthing plan is the one that makes you feel most secure and prepared for this momentous event.

While hospital births remain the most common when giving birth, other options exist, such as water births and midwife-assisted home births. Water birthing involves using a pool or warm water to aid in the labor process, and studies have found that it can reduce the length of labor and pain for those giving birth.

Midwife-assisted home births are another option; this involves hiring a midwife who can provide medical attention during the birthing process in your home. It is important to consider your options carefully and consult your doctor or midwife to ensure you find the best plan for you and your baby.

Birthing centers are an increasingly popular alternative to hospital birth in some areas. Most typically staffed by midwives, these centers offer a more natural and relaxed birthing experience with fewer interventions than a typical hospital birth.

You can expect personalized care tailored to your needs in a birthing center, including nutrition advice and comfort measures during labor. Many birth centers provide additional services such as postpartum counseling or breastfeeding support.

It is important to research the birth center that is most conveniently located to you so that you can ensure you are receiving the best care possible.

Pain management during labor and delivery is important when preparing for childbirth. One of the most popular forms of pain relief during labor is epidural anesthesia, which can provide significant pain relief by numbing the lower half of the body.

Relaxation techniques such as breathing exercises, massage therapy, visualization, and positioning changes: Relaxation techniques such as breathing exercises, massage therapy, visualization, and positioning changes can be an effective form of pain relief during labor.

The benefits of these techniques include reducing stress and tension in the body, helping the mother to control her breathing, and allowing her to focus on relaxation throughout labor. However, they may be less effective in managing severe pain or discomfort. Additionally, some positions or activities during labor may only sometimes be comfortable for mothers in more advanced stages of delivery.

Use of a birth ball: A birth ball can effectively relieve pain during labor. Benefits include helping the mother to find more comfortable positions, creating balance and stability during contractions, and reducing stress on the lower back.

However, using a birth ball may not always be ideal for women in the advanced stages of delivery, which require more support. Some forms of relaxation or positioning, such as squatting or rocking on the ball, are unsuitable for all women due to health restrictions or discomfort.

Pain medication administered through an IV or IM injection: Pain medication administered through an IV or IM injection can be helpful during labor. Benefits include the potential to reduce overall pain levels, providing a more consistent level of relief than other methods, and the ability to administer the medications quickly.

However, there are drawbacks as well. Pain medications administered through an IV or IM injection may not be suitable for all women due to health restrictions and may have negative side effects such as drowsiness. Additionally, these forms of medication can also impair a mother's ability to push effectively during delivery.

Hypnosis/hypnotherapy: Hypnosis and hypnotherapy can be beneficial during pregnancy, labor, and delivery. Benefits include relaxation, improved discomfort during labor contractions, and a sense of control while birthing.

However, some women may experience negative side effects such as increased anxiety, making it difficult to cope with pain during labor. It is also important to consult a trained professional before attempting any hypnosis or hypnotherapy due to the nature of hypnosis and trance-like states.

Water therapy (using tubs, showers, or other forms of hydrotherapy): Water therapy during pregnancy, labor, and delivery can offer many benefits.

These include relaxation and pain relief, as the water's weight helps reduce the impact of contractions on the body. Additionally, due to its natural buoyancy, water can reduce strain on joints, making it easier for pregnant women to move around comfortably.

The downside is that prolonged exposure to hot water can lead to overheating, which could harm both mother and baby. It is also important to consult with a medical professional before using any form of hydrotherapy or water therapy during pregnancy.

Transcutaneous electrical nerve stimulation (TENS): Transcutaneous electrical nerve stimulation (TENS) has been used as a form of pain relief during labor and delivery. Benefits include reducing pain intensity and helping women feel more in control of the birthing process.

However, there are potential risks associated with using TENS, such as the potential for electric shock or burning of the skin. It is important to consult with a medical professional before attempting any TENS therapy during pregnancy or labor.

Aromatherapy: Aromatherapy can be used during pregnancy, labor, and delivery to help reduce anxiety, stress, and pain. The use of essential oils can provide a calming effect, allowing expecting mothers to relax in preparation for childbirth. Some essential oils may also act as an analgesic, reducing the intensity of contractions.

The downside is that aromatherapy could produce adverse effects if used improperly due to the potency of certain oils. It is important to consult with a medical professional before attempting any aromatherapy during pregnancy or labor.

Educate Yourself

Once the delivery day arrives, it is important to stay focused and remain positive. To help ensure a successful and safe delivery, it is important to be as prepared as possible.

This includes educating yourself about the birthing process, reading up on labor and delivery procedures in books or online, attending classes, and asking questions. Aside from the mental preparation necessary for delivery day, physical preparation is also key.

Make sure to pack all your essential items, such as clothing for both mother and baby, toiletries, snacks, cameras, and chargers beforehand. Additionally, bring any insurance cards or paperwork from the doctor or hospital.

Taking the proper steps before the delivery day can help ensure everything goes according to plan when it is time for your bundle of joy to arrive!

Pack Essentials

Preparing for the delivery day is important, and packing all essential items ahead of time can help make that happen. Make sure to bring clothing for both mother and baby, toiletries, snacks, cameras, and chargers. Remember to include insurance cards or any paperwork required by your doctor or hospital.

Taking the time to pack before labor begins will ensure you are ready once it's time to go to the hospital. Having everything ready will give you peace of mind during this special day and take away some of the stress associated with giving birth.

Stay Focused and Positive

It is important to stay focused and remain positive when the delivery day arrives. Keeping your mind on the amazing result of having a healthy baby can help provide much-needed motivation during this special time.

Preparing for labor and delivery by educating yourself about the birthing process, reading up on procedures, attending classes, and asking questions can also do wonders in helping to keep your spirits high.

Focus on the beautiful outcome that awaits you instead of dreading the labor ahead. A positive outlook will make an enormous difference during this exciting but sometimes difficult journey!

Chapter 4

Preferences for Interventions

When creating your birth plan, it is important to consider your preferences about using pain relief methods or other medical interventions during labor and delivery.

Medication-Based Pain Relief

Medication-based pain relief methods are a popular choice for many women regarding pain management during labor and delivery. Here are some of the most common medication-based pain relief options available:

An epidural is a type of pain relief during labor and delivery that involves the injection of an anesthetic into the spine. This numbs the lower body, providing immediate and long-lasting pain relief. Epidurals are commonly used in hospital births, although they can also be adapted for home birth settings.

The effects of an epidural typically begin within minutes of the injection and usually last for around four to six hours after birth. Common side effects include a drop in blood pressure, itching or burning sensation along the injection site, and temporary numbness or weakness in your lower extremities.

It is important to discuss any risks, benefits, and side effects with your healthcare provider before deciding if an epidural is right for you during the labor and delivery process.

Narcotics such as morphine or fentanyl are commonly used during labor and delivery to provide short-term and more intense pain relief.

Although these medications typically begin to take effect within minutes, they can also cause side effects such as nausea, vomiting, and drowsiness. It is important to discuss the risks, benefits, and side effects with your healthcare provider before using narcotics during labor and delivery.

When choosing a narcotic for use during labor and delivery, it is essential to consider the dosage and how quickly the effects will wear off. You may choose ongoing pain relief instead of a one-time dose depending on your specific needs.

Nitrous Oxide (Laughing Gas)

Nitrous oxide is a type of medication-based pain relief often used during labor and delivery. It provides short bursts of pain relief while helping relax the patient, allowing them to focus on the task. The nitrous oxide is delivered in a mixture of 50% oxygen and 50% nitrous oxide through a mask or face mask.

The effects of nitrous oxide typically begin immediately and last throughout use. Common side effects include nausea and dizziness, which usually dissipate after use. Be sure to speak with your healthcare provider about any risks, benefits, and side effects before deciding if nitrous oxide is appropriate for you during labor and delivery.

Non-Medication Based Interventions

Non-medication-based interventions such as vacuum extraction or forceps delivery can be used during labor and delivery to help reduce pain and aid in the baby's delivery. Here are some of the most common non-medication options available.

Vacuum Extraction

Vacuum extraction is used during labor and delivery to aid the baby's delivery. This technique uses a suction cup device that attaches to the baby's head and helps to guide it out of the birth canal. Vacuum extraction is typically performed when contractions are not strong enough or when the baby is too large for a natural delivery.

There can be risks associated with vacuum extraction, including scalp trauma, scalp swelling or infection, damage to the baby's skull, facial nerve injury, and an increased risk of postpartum hemorrhage.

It is important to discuss any potential risks, benefits, and side effects with your healthcare provider before deciding if vacuum extraction is right for you during labor and delivery.

Forceps Delivery

Forceps delivery is a type of assisted delivery that involves the insertion of two metal tongs into the birth canal to help guide and rotate the baby into an easier position for delivery.

It can be used to safely deliver a baby when there are difficulties with contractions or if the mother is exhausted from pushing. Risks associated with forceps delivery include:

- Bruising or trauma to the baby's scalp.
- Facial nerve injury.
- Temporary dental trauma.
- Cranium damage.
- Increased risk of postpartum hemorrhage.

Cervical Ripening

Cervical ripening is a procedure used during labor and delivery to help soften the cervix and make it easier for labor to progress. This technique involves the insertion of a catheter or balloon into the cervix for several hours, which helps to soften and widen the cervix so that delivery can be achieved more easily.

Cervical ripening can help speed up labor and reduce the need for medical interventions such as forceps delivery or Cesarean section (C-section). Risks associated with cervical ripening may include infection, preterm birth, uterine rupture, and an increased risk of postpartum hemorrhage.

Supplies and Equipment Needed

Childbirth is an incredible and unique experience that comes with a range of emotions. Having the proper supplies and equipment can help make the birth experience more comfortable for both mom and baby and increase safety during labor.

Different supplies and equipment are necessary for a hospital or birthing center birth, a home birth, and comfort items for both mom and baby.

- Increased safety during labor.
- Improved comfort throughout the entire labor process.
- Ensuring that both mom and baby have everything they need at the delivery time.
- A more positive overall birth experience.

When preparing for childbirth, it is important to have the right supplies and equipment. Here is a list of essential items needed for a hospital or birthing center birth:

- Labor gowns
- Slippers

- Sanitary pads
- Massage tools such as tennis balls or an inflatable tub pillow
- Hair ties and clips
- Towels
- Nursing bras and breast pads
- Water bottle
- Lip balm
- Change of clothes
- Mesh underwear

For a home birth, additional items may be needed, including:

- A birthing pool or tub with liner and thermometer.
- Containers for storing water before use in the tub/pool.
- Birthing stool or ball to aid in different labor positions.
- Pillows for extra comfort during labor.

Finally, some items can help make mom more comfortable after delivery. These include:

- Nursing pillows or cushions to help ease feeding position discomfort
- Breastfeeding covers and blankets to maintain privacy while nursing.
- Nipple cream and shields to soothe sore nipples.
- Diapers and wipes for changing baby.
- Soft blankets, clothing, and burp cloths for swaddling and cleaning up after feeding.

These are just a few of the essential supplies needed for childbirth. It is important to speak with your healthcare provider about any additional items that may.

Chapter 5

Understanding the Three Stages of Labor

If you're a first-time dad, you may wonder what the three stages of labor are and what you should be doing during this time. While every birth is different, there are general guidelines that can help you prepare for and support your wife during labor.

We'll cover the basics of each stage of labor and what you can do to help your wife through it.

Labor is a stressful experience for mothers-to-be, and understanding the journey through the three stages of labor can help you prepare better. The latent phase consists of contractions that are becoming more frequent but aren't usually too intense.

This phase can last up to several hours or even days. Afterward, the active phase begins with contractions that occur more often and become much stronger.

Finally, the transitional phase is the most difficult, where contractions come at their most intense and regular intervals before delivering the baby soon after. Educating yourself on the process beforehand can make it less daunting when that day arrives.

The Latent Phase

The latent phase is when the contractions begin to pick up and become more regular. This is a good time to start walking around or taking a bath to help ease the pain.

During the latent phase of labor, your contractions may not be painful at first, but they will increase in intensity and frequency. This is a great time to get up and walk around or take a warm bath - all those extra steps help alleviate some discomfort. Of course, you should also talk to your OBGYN about any other methods that you can use for relief.

One thing you should keep in mind is that when the time comes, pain management might become a real game-changer!

As a new dad, there are many ways you can help your wife during the latent phase of her pregnancy. Here are some tips:

- Be patient and understanding: The latent phase can last several weeks, and your wife may feel uncomfortable and anxious. Be there for her, listen to her concerns, and offer your support.
- Help her relax: Encourage your wife to take breaks and rest when needed. Offer to give her a massage, run a bath, or practice relaxation exercises together.
- Be involved in the birth plan: Work with your wife to create a birth plan that meets your needs and preferences. Attend childbirth education classes and discuss any concerns or questions you may have.
- Take care of household chores: As your wife's due date approaches, she may have less energy and mobility. Take on extra household chores, such as cooking, cleaning, and laundry, to ease her burden.
- Stay informed: Learn about the signs of labor and when to call the doctor. Keep your phone with you always in case your wife goes into labor.

Remember, every pregnancy is different, and your wife may have specific needs and preferences. The most important thing is to be there for her, listen to her, and offer your support whenever possible.

The Active Phase

The active phase is when the contractions are strongest and most frequent. This is when you should start pushing if you have not already.

Labor contractions typically start slowly and become increasingly intense as the labor progresses. When you enter the active phase of labor, your contractions reach their hardest point, occurring more frequently and lasting longer.

So if you still need to start pushing, the active phase is the time to do it! Pushing can be lengthy, so do not worry if you feel like you are at it for a while. When people think of labor, they often overlook this stage—many assume once the contractions begin, delivery is imminent—but it represents a crucial step on your baby's journey into the world.

It is important to note that the decision to start pushing during labor is up to the healthcare provider and the birthing person. While the active phase of labor typically involves strong and frequent contractions, pushing may not always begin immediately at this stage.

The timing and method of pushing may vary depending on the individual's birthing plan, the baby's position, and the healthcare provider's guidance. It is important to communicate with your healthcare provider and follow their guidance during labor and delivery.

There are several steps you can take to support your wife during the active phase of labor.

- Encourage and motivate her: Use positive language to encourage and motivate your wife throughout the active phase of labor. Remind her of her strength and how well she is doing.
- Help her manage pain: Offer to help your wife use pain management techniques, such as breathing exercises, massage, or hot/cold compresses. You can also ask the healthcare provider about other pain relief options.
- Keep her comfortable: Help your wife get into comfortable positions and provide pillows or other items to support her. Offer to adjust the room temperature or lighting to her liking.

- Provide emotional support: Be a calming and reassuring presence for your wife. Listen to her concerns and provide emotional support throughout the active phase of labor.
- Communicate with healthcare providers: Keep your healthcare provider informed about changes in your wife's condition or how she feels. Advocate for her needs and preferences.

The Transitional Phase

The transitional phase of labor is like a wild rollercoaster - the difficulties come quickly, but it is all worth it in the end! This is usually the shortest and most intense part of labor, where your baby begins to descend into the birth canal.

It can be an overwhelming experience as your body adjusts to the changing speed, discomfort, and intense sensations. However, if you focus on your breathing and trust your body's natural ability to give birth, you will get through this phase with loads of support from your birthing team!

During the transition period of labor, you can provide emotional support to his wife by:

- Reminding her of her strength: The transition period can be intense and emotionally challenging. Encourage your wife by reminding her of her strength and how well she is doing.
- Listening to her: Be active and respond to your wife's emotional needs. She may need to express her fears, concerns, or anxieties, and it is important to provide a supportive ear.
- Offering words of affirmation: Provide affirmation and encouragement to your wife. You can express your love for her and your belief in her ability to give birth.
- Providing physical comfort: Help your wife get into comfortable positions and provide comfort measures such as massage or hot/cold compresses.
- Being patient and understanding: The transition period can be unpre-

dictable and may take longer than expected. Be patient and understanding with your wife as she goes through this process.

It is also important to be aware of any emotional signs that may indicate your wife needs extra support, such as increased anxiety, agitation, or feeling overwhelmed. If you notice these signs, you must communicate with your healthcare provider and provide additional emotional support to your wife.

So, there you have it, the three stages of labor and what to expect during each one. Remember that every birth is different, so take your time with the details. The most important thing is to stay calm and focus on safely bringing your baby into the world.

Here are some other ideas for how you can support your wife during labor, regardless of the phase:

· Keep your wife hydrated and offer her snacks or small meals as the healthcare provider allows.
· Help create a calm and soothing environment in the delivery room by playing music or dimming the lights.
· Use touch and physical contact to provide comfort and support.
· Take breaks as needed to rest and recharge but remain available to your wife as much as possible.
· Be open and flexible to changes in the labor and delivery process and adjust your support as needed.
· Capture special moments with photos or videos, if allowed and desired by your wife.
· Celebrate and cherish the birth of your child together as a family.

Breathing During Active Labor

As a wife, you want to do everything you can to support your wife. One of the best ways you can help is by providing assistance with breathing, which helps manage the pain and prepare her for delivery.

This next section discusses the benefits of having a wife present during active labor, different breathing techniques available to help manage pain, and what you can do as a wife to assist your wife when using these techniques.

One of the best ways you can help is by providing assistance with breathing, which helps manage the pain and prepare her for delivery.

You can provide emotional support, physical reassurance, and help with breathing exercises which can all help to ease any anxiety or fear your wife may have. You can usually be in the delivery room and help establish a sense of connection and security, which helps reduce stress levels. Being present during labor also gives you an even deeper appreciation and understanding of the birthing process.

You have a key role to play in the labor and delivery of your child. Being present in the delivery room with her creates a sense of connection and security that can help ease her anxiety or fear.

Remember that teaching breathing techniques can be incredibly helpful for both of you - it helps manage pain and gives you an even deeper appreciation and understanding of the birthing process.

Focus on each breath, which can help create a sense of relaxation and remove her discomfort.

Different breathing techniques like progressive muscle relaxation, diaphragmatic breathing, and abdominal breathing are available, which you can learn from classes or books offered by hospitals.

Progressive muscle relaxation involves tensing and systematically releasing each muscle group until the body is fully relaxed.

- Start by tensing the muscles in your feet and hold for a few seconds
- Slowly move up your body, tensing each muscle group as she goes
- Take a few deep breaths in between each muscle group
- Relax the muscles until she feels release
- Move up her body until all muscle groups are relaxed

Diaphragmatic breathing: also known as "belly breathing," encourages taking slow, deep breaths with your diaphragm instead of shallow breaths with your chest.

- Place one hand on your stomach, just below your rib cage.
- Take a deep breath in through your nose and feel the air move from your abdomen to your chest.
- Exhale slowly, pushing the air out of your diaphragm.
- Repeat this process a few times.
- Focus on easing any tension in the body while breathing.

Abdominal breathing: requires relaxing the abdomen so that each breath can travel deeper into your abdomen than normal.

- Sit in a comfortable position and bring your attention to your breath
- Place one hand on your abdomen and the other on your heart
- Slowly breathe in through your nose, drawing the air into your abdomen. Feel the abdomen rise as you inhale
- Exhale slowly out of your mouth, allowing all tension to release from the body
- Focus on each breath, keeping the mind clear and still
- Practice for several minutes or until you feel relaxed

Other things to think about:

- Massage her back, feet, and other areas of discomfort
- Respect her need for quiet and minimize distractions
- Suggest she take breaks between contractions if necessary

For extra support during labor, consider making a physical reminder for your wife to help her focus on her breathing exercises.

Hang a list of reminders in the birthing room like "Pause and Breath," "Relax Your Shoulders," or "Focus On Your Breath" to help keep her relaxed and focused.

You can also get creative and make special personalized reminders to encourage your wife, such as hanging posters with positive sayings, drawing pictures representing relaxation, and placing calming scents like lavender around the room.

A supportive atmosphere will make it easier for your wife to relax and concentrate on her breathing exercises.

Chapter 6

Advocating For Your Wife

Childbirth and postpartum care are important and exciting experiences for expectant mothers and their families. The presence of an advocate in the delivery room can provide comfort, support, and peace of mind during these moments.

Fathers also play a key role in childbirth and postpartum care by providing physical and emotional support to both the mother and baby. We will explore the benefits of having an advocate with you in the delivery room and the dad's role during childbirth and postpartum care.

During Delivery

- Provide support: An advocate during delivery can provide physical and emotional support for the expectant mother and her wife by helping to monitor vital signs, address any medical concerns, offer guidance, answer questions, and provide reassurance.
- Minimize stress: An advocate can help lessen the stress and anxiety associated with childbirth by providing a calming presence in the delivery room that helps keep everyone focused on delivering a healthy baby.
- Assist with decisions: An advocate can help expectant parents make informed decisions about their delivery plan based on their circumstances and preferences.

- Help maintain comfort level: An advocate can also help maintain a comfortable environment in the delivery room by aiding with positioning, massage techniques, music selection, or other comforts that the expectant mother may desire during labor and delivery.

You have an important role in pregnancy and childbirth. Providing emotional support, practical guidance, and physical assistance before, during, and after labor is essential for both your wife and your baby—not to mention building a strong bond between you and your newborn.

Before the big day arrives, it's important that you attend prenatal visits with your wife. This is the perfect opportunity for you to learn about the labor process and potential complications.

This is the time to plan ahead—stock up on diapers, purchase supplies like bottles or car seats, and help your wife create her birth plan.

Once delivery starts, you can be an advocate for both your wife and child by listening to their medical team's instructions while still advocating for their needs during the delivery.

Afterward, there are plenty of post-delivery responsibilities that will require your immediate attention—like helping care for mom and baby upon returning home from the hospital.

Whatever stage of pregnancy or childbirth you're in—remember, there are many ways as a father that you can play an important role in bringing new life into this world!

This includes providing physical comfort through massage techniques or ensuring that the mother's needs are met in any way possible.

You also play a crucial role in monitoring vital signs while helping your wife cope with any pain or anxiety they may feel throughout labor. After delivery, you must help provide emotional support to your wife as she recovers from childbirth.

This includes caring for the baby during nursing sessions or diaper changes and assisting with housework tasks when needed. It is also important for you to be present during follow-up doctor appointments so that they can discuss any concerns your wife may have regarding her health or the baby's care.

Recognizing Signs of Stress

Other signs of stress or exhaustion include feeling overwhelmed by pain, having difficulty making decisions regarding care options, or experiencing extreme mood swings. You should comfort your wife and advocate for her if needed.

As a father, it is important for you to recognize signs of stress and exhaustion in your wife during the birthing process. Fatigue is a common symptom that mothers experience due to restricted movement and lack of rest throughout labor. You can help your wife stay strong by encouraging and supporting them through this period.

Don't be afraid to take the initiative—offer words of affirmation and comfort when they are feeling tired and overwhelmed. Providing moral support during childbirth will have a lasting impact in strengthening the bond between you and your new baby!

It is also important to prepare emotionally by utilizing relaxation techniques such as deep breathing or meditation before childbirth and recognizing signs of stress or exhaustion in your wife during the birthing process so you can offer comfort when needed.

Being a father means being there for both mother and baby every step of the way - something that will benefit both parents immensely!

Preparing for Emergencies

While it is impossible to plan for all emergencies, being aware and prepared can go a long way. One of the first steps is identifying potential risks. It is important to assess your wife's health history and be aware of it if you plan on playing an active role during this entire process. Consult with a medical professional and understand complications.

Investigating local resources and facilities should be considered when identifying potential risks in a delivery room situation; this means understanding which hospitals have neonatal intensive care units and nearby birthing centers with midwives or doulas who can provide additional support during labor.

When assessing the mother's health history in preparation for delivery, understand and know about her existing medical conditions. She may be experiencing so much pain and so focused on the immediate what is happening now that she may not even think of certain items such as what kind of medication, she is taking to treat any pre-existing conditions. You can be her voice in those moments.

This includes any allergies and prior medical treatments she may have had, as well as a family history of any conditions or diseases that may impact the labor process.

This is especially important if underlying health issues could cause difficulties during labor. Understanding the possible complications related to deliveries and the options available in an emergency is also beneficial.

This includes knowing the signs of distress during labor or delivery, being aware of diverse types of interventions such as medication or surgical procedures and having access to trained personnel who can handle these situations.

Establishing a support system for labor and delivery is also essential for mitigating potential risks. Having close friends or family nearby to provide emotional support can be invaluable and have access to trained professionals knowledgeable about the labor process.

Many hospitals have lactation consultants or childbirth educators who can assist with the various aspects of birthing.

Additionally, finding organizations that offer postpartum resources, such as support groups and counseling services, can prove beneficial after the baby is born—establishing this type of supportive network before labor can make all the difference in identifying potential risks and providing the best care possible during one of the most important moments in life.

Developing a communication plan for labor and delivery is essential for staying connected with loved ones and providing prompt updates about the birthing process. Make sure family and friends are aware of hospital policies beforehand to know if, when, and how they can be involved during pregnancy.

It is wise to have access to various forms of communication if cell phone service is unavailable or unreliable.

Lastly, having an alternate form of contact information that others can easily access in an emergency. Establishing these protocols will allow everything to run more smoothly during labor and delivery.

- Inform family and friends of hospital policies regarding their involvement during labor and delivery.
- Consider investing in a landline or two-way radio for better communication if cell phone service is unreliable.
- Keep an alternate form of contact information that others can easily access in an emergency.
- Compile a list of important numbers, such as your local hospital after hours line and regular business line, your wife's primary care number, and healthcare practitioners, who should be contacted during a crisis during labor and delivery.
- Share the contact information with trusted individuals who will not be present at the birthing process but must be kept informed about the progress.
- Establish a protocol for how and when updates should be shared so that everyone remains on the same page throughout the process.

Dealing with breathing or bleeding issues in the delivery room can be intimidating, so it's important to come prepared. Have a plan for medical emergencies and know what steps should be taken if complications arise.

Understanding Types of Births

It is important for fathers-to-be to understand the different types of births and why each may be necessary. Knowing about potential complications such as low amniotic fluid or breech position can help fathers prepare to make informed decisions in any scenario.

In addition, familiarity with the labor and delivery process will enable dads to provide emotional and physical support during a time that can be stressful and painful for the mother. As such, dads-to-be needs to be informed on all aspects of childbirth.

Vaginal delivery is the most common form of childbirth and typically the most preferred option. It involves the mother pushing the baby out of her body and through the birth canal. Typically, a vaginal delivery is only done when there are no medical complications, such as low amniotic fluid or breech position, and when labor has progressed to the active phase.

Vaginal deliveries often result in shorter labor times and fewer post-delivery complications for both mother and baby. This form of birth is also favored due to its reduced risk of infection, which makes it a safer option than other types of births.

Sometimes, a mother may opt for a Cesarean section (C-section) due to medical complications or for the baby's safety. A C-section involves an incision in the abdomen and uterus to deliver the baby.

This is often done when labor has not progressed enough or when potential complications could put the baby at risk, such as low amniotic fluid, breech position, abnormal fetal development, or multiple births.

In addition, a C-section can be performed when the mother has certain conditions, such as high blood pressure or diabetes.

A C-section may be scheduled in advance if a doctor believes there may be medical complications that prevent successful vaginal delivery.

This is typically decided after consulting with the mother and monitoring any changes in the baby's health or development. In some cases, a mother may request a C-section even if there are no medical complications, as it can give her more control over the time of birth, avoid potential complications during labor, or for other personal reasons.

A medical emergency C-section may be necessary if complications during labor or delivery put the mother and baby's health and safety at risk. This can include placental abruption, umbilical cord prolapse, or a baby in distress. In these cases, the C-section is performed quickly to ensure the safety of both mother and baby.

A team typically decides to perform a C-section, doctors, and nurses in consultation with the mother. Factors such as the baby's health and development, any potential risks to the mother or baby during labor or delivery, the mother's preferences, and other potential medical complications that could arise are all considered when making the decision.

The term "C-section" refers to the type of incision made during the procedure, which is a curved incision in the mother's abdomen, resembling the letter "C."

The practice of performing a C-section was first documented by the ancient Romans and has evolved over centuries into its modern form. The name is derived from Latin terminology meaning "to cut open" or "cut down." This name was eventually adopted in English medical circles and spread to other languages.

The first recorded use of a C-section dates back to 1500 BC, with evidence of the procedure being performed by the ancient Egyptians. C-sections were refined over time, becoming more commonplace in the 19th century with the advent of anesthesia and antibiotics.

By the mid-20th century, C-sections were increasingly used as an alternative to natural childbirth. Today, they are routine, and the safe procedure is often used when labor or delivery is difficult or dangerous for either mother or baby.

As a father, you can play an important role in supporting your wife during the birthing process.

When you're informed about the delivery type, you'll be better equipped to provide emotional and physical support before, during, and after childbirth. Information about delivery type will also help you become familiar with any potential risks associated with the procedure.

You can be part of the decision-making process by understanding what types of deliveries are available and when each may be necessary for the health and safety of mother and baby. Being informed about delivery type will also give you greater confidence in your wife's care and a deeper understanding of the birthing process overall.

Being present in the delivery room while your wife is giving birth is one of the most emotionally powerful moments many fathers will experience.

It is a joyous yet nerve-wracking time, full of apprehension and anticipation. The birthing process can be difficult for both mother and father.

Onlookers may not understand the magnitude of emotion a dad feels — from fear for his wife's safety and worrying about what kind of father he'll be to pure, overwhelmed happiness when their baby is born.

For new dads, it can be hard to feel useful during labor, but providing a calming presence through words of encouragement and physical comfort can be incredibly beneficial for both mom and baby.

Additionally, dads should take time throughout pregnancy to mentally prepare themselves for this life-changing event alone. It's important to remember that all birthing experiences are unique; there are no right or wrong ways to feel like an expecting father.

All emotions should be expressed and validated regardless of how irrational they may seem. Ultimately, a dad's supportive presence during this special time will never go unnoticed by his wife or child.

As a new dad, you can reduce your stress levels during labor and delivery by staying informed about the process.

Learn as much as possible about what to expect before, during, and after delivery - such as when to come to the hospital, what to do if there are any complications, or how best to provide physical comfort through massage or counterpressure.

Additionally, stay involved in discussions with the medical staff and ask questions whenever necessary. By being informed and involved, you will better grasp things that may arise during labor and delivery, which can lead to fewer surprises and less stress during this significant time of life.

You can still be there and provide support for your wife's labor experience, even if you cannot physically be there. Whether through phone calls, video chats, text messages, or helping out with household tasks like grocery shopping and errands, you can still make a significant impact.

Keeping informed by talking to the medical staff and asking questions will also ensure you are up-to-date on how things are progressing.

Although being present in person may not be possible, your wife will surely appreciate your dedication and thoughtfulness regarding her labor and delivery.

Even if you can't be there in person, dads can make a difference by checking in on their wife through phone calls or video chats. Dads can also show their support by offering to help with household tasks such as grocery shopping and errands.

Furthermore, fathers should keep in touch with the medical staff and ask questions, so they are always up-to-date on how their wife is progressing. By taking part in small acts of support even when they cannot be there physically, dads can still significantly impact during labor and delivery.

Inducing Labor Past 40 Weeks?

As your wife enters her 40th week of pregnancy, it's normal for both of you to feel anxious. While childbirth can be an exciting and magical time, it can also cause anxiety as the due date passes.

If your wife has entered her 40th week or beyond, inducing labor may be necessary for the safety of the mother and baby. Learn more about why labor induction is sometimes necessary and the associated risks.

As a first-time father, you may wonder what to expect regarding your wife's due date. While the due date is often considered more of a suggestion than an exact appointment, most babies are born between 38 and 42 weeks. If your baby arrives after the due date passes, this is perfectly normal.

Inducing labor at 40 weeks gestation can be safe for both mom and baby, although risks are involved. Before making any decisions about induction, be sure to talk with the doctor about the pros and cons to make an informed decision.

As any expectant parent can tell you, the wait for labor and childbirth is sometimes as exciting as it is nerve-wracking. Nowadays, doctors can give pregnant mothers the option of inducing labor if they have passed their due date to reduce the potential risks of prolonged pregnancy.

Because it's a medically administered procedure, there will always be the possibility that the inducement of labor doesn't go according to plan or could, in some cases, cause an even greater risk of complications for both mother and child.

However, in most cases, labor induction is safe and beneficial for medical reasons. Considering discomfort and health risks is a part of this process and helps inform the discussion between your wife and her doctor in making the best medical decision.

Making an informed decision about induction is important for you and your wife. Ask questions about the best practices for inducing labor, such as the timing and procedure used.

Be sure to discuss any other medical considerations related to your situation. Finally, consider any emotional concerns you and your wife may have about induction so that you can make an informed decision together.

Inducing labor at 40 weeks can have several risks associated with it. These risks include an increased chance of Cesarean delivery, infection, or even umbilical cord complications.

Additionally, there is the potential for increased pain during labor and delivery due to contractions coming more often than normal. There may also be a risk of fetal distress or prematurity if the labor is induced too early. It's important to discuss these risks with the doctor so that you can make an informed decision about induction.

Inducing labor can have a variety of outcomes depending on the individual situation. Generally, an induction will result in a successful vaginal delivery. In some cases, an induction may help avoid a Cesarean delivery if the baby is in distress.

Pros of inducing labor at 40 weeks:

- It can help avoid a Cesarean delivery if the baby is in distress
- Labor is usually shorter and more tolerable than waiting for labor to start naturally
- There's less risk of prematurity or post-term pregnancy.

Cons of inducing labor at 40 weeks:

- Increased chance of infection or umbilical cord complications due to the induction process
- Many mothers that are induced with medications take longer and cause more discomfort than women that start on their own

· Increased risk of Cesarean delivery compared to letting labor happen naturally.

The best practices for inducing labor include determining the right time to induce, understanding the risks and benefits associated with induction, and discussing with the doctor what type of medication will be used. It's important to consider important conditions such as gestational age, cervical dilation, fetal lung maturity, and fetal position before beginning the induction process. It is important to note that inducing labor with certain medications may take longer than others and cause more discomfort. Monitoring the baby's heart rate during labor is also necessary to ensure safe delivery.

Additional medical considerations that should be considered when inducing labor include the mother's health history and any preexisting conditions, such as diabetes or hypertension.

Other considerations include ensuring adequate hydration for the mother and monitoring her vital signs, such as blood pressure and temperature. Additionally, it is important to consider any medications the mother is taking and their potential effects on labor.

Emotional concerns associated with labor induction can include anxiety and fear surrounding the process, as well as guilt or disappointment over not being able to give birth naturally. It is important for both the mother and father to discuss their concerns with a doctor before proceeding with an induction.

The mother needs support throughout the process - this could be an attending physician, nurse, or family member. Finally, practicing relaxation techniques and determining strategies to manage stress during labor is helpful.

If you're about to be induced, the best thing you can do for yourself is to prepare for the unexpected. During induction, complications such as an insufficient cervix or fetal distress are possible - though rare - and can be difficult to anticipate.

Should any complications arise, it's important to have a medical professional present who is experienced with induction and can provide in-depth advice.

If a complication is more serious and requires extra care or management, the doctor will also help you decide whether a cesarean section might be necessary.

When it comes to managing potential problems during or after induction, being proactive is key: talk to the doctor beforehand and research everything to ensure that you have all the facts at hand if anything comes up.

Chapter 7

Choosing the Baby's Name

Are you having trouble choosing the perfect baby's name? Don't worry; you're not alone. It's one of the most common pieces of advice new dads get: pick a name you and your wife can agree on. But how do you do that?

Here are a few tips to help you choose the perfect baby's name without fighting with your wife. These will help make the process a little easier for you!

Considering a name for a baby can be an overwhelming process. It's important to decide what kind of name you want – a traditional, unique, family tradition, something ethnic – before looking through lists.

Remember that the specific name won't define your child's character or future success; it's more about finding something that matches and expresses their identity.

Consider the pronunciation and nickname potential when narrowing down your choice. Also, remember that your baby will grow into their name over time, so trust your instincts on the one that feels right!

Finding baby names that you and your partner agree on can be quite challenging! But with a bit of communication and creative brainstorming, it is possible to come up with a few options that you and your partner like.

Think of what kind of name best reflects the personality of your little bundle of joy, or take a trip down memory lane by using family names. As long as the name has meaning to both of you, it will surely bring happiness - even if it takes you a while to decide!

Stay calm when deciding which name to use for a product or project. Instead, move forward with a handful of the names you like the most and try them out in different contexts.

See how they look written down side-by-side, how people respond to them when mentioned casually, or find other creative ways to see which one best fits your overall product or project. Testing the names can help ensure you feel confident about how your audience will receive them.

It can be frustrating when you and your partner can't figure out what to name a new baby. When it feels like no matter what you suggest, nothing sits right with the both of you, then take some advice – reach out to family and friends for their opinion.

Getting input from outside sources with different perspectives will spark some fresh ideas that will get you back on track in finding a name perfect for your little one. Plus, who knows? You may even find that your friends and family offer up the dream name that clicks with both of you!

Stay attached when naming the newest addition to your family! With all the options, staying open-minded and looking at different sources for inspiration is best. Be bold and change names if you realize it isn't the perfect fit for your child - chances are you'll find something even better once you keep searching!

It's important to remember that although many people might have their opinion about your choice, it's up to you and your family to pick what works best for everyone. Let yourself enjoy exploring all possibilities and choose the name that has a special meaning for you.

Embrace this exciting time in your life and have a lot of fun! There are endless possibilities ahead and many things to explore and discover.

Whether traveling to a new place, learning a new skill or hobby, or just playing some games with friends – we only live once, so why not make the most of it?

Make sure to take the time to cherish all of these experiences, as these are often the moments you will look back on fondly. Enjoy yourself, and be confident that this period of your life is worth remembering!

To Circumcise or Not

As a new father, you may wonder whether or not to circumcise your baby son. Both decisions have pros and cons; ultimately, it is up to you to decide what is best for your family. Here are some things to consider when making your decision.

Circumcision can provide several benefits to those who choose to do it, such as reducing the risk of urinary tract infections, making hygiene easier, and causing less pain during erections. For young children, UTIs can be particularly difficult to manage and can lead to more serious health risks further down the line.

Easier hygiene is another major advantage of circumcision; simply put, it's easier for men to keep their genital area clean when there are fewer places for bacteria or dirt to hide. Lastly, males who are circumcised may experience less discomfort during erections because the foreskin is no longer pulling against the penis.

It may sound like a small detail, but having erections without pain or irritation greatly affects overall sexual health and satisfaction.

Despite its potential benefits, circumcision does have several cons. Most obviously, there is the potential for serious complications arising from the surgery itself due to infection, excessive bleeding, or other issues, though complications are very rare.

Loss of sensation can also occur with circumcision as there could be too much skin removed in the process; this could then cause lasting problems with sexual satisfaction in adulthood.

Finally, pain is another con to consider, as no anesthesia or analgesics are used during the procedure - though it is incredibly brief - and babies may experience physical and psychological trauma from it.

Ultimately, weighing up the pros and cons of circumcision should be judged individually depending on one's religious, cultural, or personal beliefs.

When it decides whether or not to circumcise your son, it is ultimately one that the parents should make after giving careful consideration.

This is a serious matter, and all available information should be considered to help you to make an informed choice. There are opinions and facts to consider from each side, but the decision of what will ultimately happen rests on the parents' shoulders.

Both options have potential risks and benefits, and it is important for those considering this option to research these factors further before making a final decision.

If you do decide to circumcise your son, make sure to choose a reputable doctor and follow all aftercare instructions carefully.

Deciding to circumcise your son can be daunting, but you want to ensure that any doctor performing the procedure is highly reputable.

Do your research! Ask your pediatrician or another doctor who they would recommend, read reviews and make sure that this doctor is up-to-date on all safety protocols.

Once the procedure is over, follow all aftercare instructions very closely - trust your doctor's expertise and take their advice seriously. Even if it seems tedious, do whatever it takes to ensure your son's healing period is as hassle-free as possible!

Plan for Childcare After Delivery

Congratulations on your upcoming bundle of joy! But the journey doesn't end once the baby arrives. Careful planning for postpartum childcare is essential to ensure a smooth transition and a successful parenting experience.

From breastfeeding support and bonding time with your newborn to financial planning and making sure someone's always around to lend an extra helping hand, having a plan before delivery can make all the difference. Here are some tips for planning childcare after delivery.

Planning for childcare before delivery can be challenging. y, identifying available childcare options in your area before delivery may prove difficult if you're unfamiliar with local services or need help knowing where to start looking.

It can also be overwhelming to compare and contrast providers or programs to determine which is best for you and your family. Finding appropriate care that fits your budget is another challenge for many parents.

- Start researching childcare options before delivery: Take the time to research available childcare options in your area and compare them to find the best fit for your family. Look into providers, programs, support groups, nanny services, and any other options that may be available.
- Decide on a budget for childcare: Determine what you can afford for childcare and create a budget for it. Consider factors like hourly rates or monthly payments, special discounts, or flexible payment plans that may be available.
- Ask for help from family and friends: If you have family or friends with children who need care, reach out to them and ask if they know of any reliable programs or providers nearby. They may even be able to provide care themselves, depending on their availability.
- Plan ahead to secure resources: Once you've found a suitable program or provider that fits your budget, secure their services as soon as possible to take advantage of availability issues or scheduling conflicts.
- Establish routines before delivery to help make the postpartum period much smoother and easier when the baby arrives. Having some structure will also help make childcare easier to manage over time.

After delivery, there are several different types of childcare available for parents to choose from. These include daycare centers, nannies, babysitters, au pairs, and in-home care. Each has its advantages and disadvantages as well as different costs.

Daycare centers typically offer an organized environment with a large staff and multiple rooms for children to play in.

The cost of daycare will depend on the type of services offered and whether it's full or part-time care. Nannies can provide more personalized attention and flexible hours than daycare centers but often come at a higher cost.

They also require specialized training and certifications that may increase their fees. Babysitters are usually less expensive than nannies, but they provide a different level of consistency due to changing schedules.

Au pairs also provide a personal touch, but they sometimes come with additional costs, such as language classes or transport fees.

In-home care is a great option for families who need occasional assistance with childminding duties or overnight supervision while they sleep. This type of care may be provided by family members or friends who aren't certified professionals but can provide the necessary support.

Physical Strain on New Dads

New fathers often underestimate the physical and emotional toll of bringing a new baby into their lives. Still, the reality is that new dads can experience considerable strain in the weeks and months after delivery.

Fatherhood is a life-changing experience that can be both exciting and overwhelming. Becoming a parent brings new responsibilities and challenges, especially when the baby arrives. The transition to fatherhood can be particularly daunting for dads as they often receive inadequate support in their parenting journey.

Research has shown that when dads receive support during this critical transition period, it positively impacts their emotional well-being and strengthens family relationships. It is essential for fathers to feel supported and empowered as they adjust to their new roles and responsibilities as parents.

Fatherhood can bring about several physical changes for new dads, often due to the pressure of a changing lifestyle. New fathers may experience fatigue, stress, poor sleep, and decreased physical activity. Too often, these changes are overlooked in favor of focusing on the baby's needs which can be detrimental to their well-being.

Other physical strains on dads may include:

- Muscle tension from carrying infants or strollers.
- Back strain from constantly bending down.
- Pains from lifting heavy objects like cribs and car seats.

New dads can also have difficulties concentrating or staying focused as they juggle responsibilities at home and work. Men need to watch out for any signs of physical strain to ensure they do not suffer over time.

Becoming a father is a life-altering experience that can be exhilarating yet daunting. New fathers are often unprepared for parenthood's overwhelming mental, emotional, and physical demands. Sleep deprivation, anxiety, and depression are just some of the emotional challenges new dads face in their transition to fatherhood.

Sleep deprivation is common among fathers as newborns often wake up throughout the night—a phenomenon called "parental sleep disruption"—and interfere with the parent's ability to rest or recuperate.

Lack of sleep can lead to exhaustion and irritability, which can strain relationships and make it harder for new dads to meet their daily responsibilities.

Anxiety may also accompany the transition from work mode to dad mode as men grapple with feelings of responsibility for another human being.

This heightened concern can lead to worries about finances or providing for the family's needs, both short and long-term; fears about parenting effectively; and pressures of balancing work with fatherhood.

Finally, depression is not uncommon among new dads due to stress caused by lack of sleep combined with social isolation from changes in usual activities like going out with friends or engaging in hobbies.

New fathers need to be mindful of their emotions and take steps toward addressing any mental health concerns they may have during this crucial period in their lives.

Preparing for fatherhood can be a daunting experience, as men often feel inadequately supported during this transition period.

That's why it is so important for new dads to have strong support networks of family, friends, and professionals in place before they become a parent. Having family members to lean on can provide comfort and help new fathers adjust to their new responsibilities.

Grandparents, sisters, brothers, and other relatives can help fathers with practical matters such as childcare and housekeeping and lend an encouraging ear when needed.

It's also beneficial for new dads to reach out to their peers who are also transitioning into parenthood—with the emergence of social media, forming virtual peer groups has become increasingly easy. Friends are also a great source of support for new fathers.

Whether catching up over coffee or venting about parenting struggles in private group chats, having people you trust can make the journey to fatherhood much easier. Having these sorts of networks available can make it easier for men to process their emotions without feeling embarrassed or judged.

Seeking professional assistance from doctors, counselors, or therapists can provide insights into better managing the physical and mental changes that come with becoming a dad.

Working with an expert allows you to get tailored advice and an opportunity to reflect on your feelings openly and honestly – which is often difficult in one's day-to-day life.

Family, friends, and experts play an important role in helping new fathers better prepare for fatherhood by providing practical advice and emotional support throughout this life-changing experience.

New fathers face many physical and emotional challenges as they transition into parenthood. Becoming a dad is an overwhelming experience, and although it has its joys, it can also bring with it physical exhaustion, anxiety, and depression.

Men must build strong support networks consisting of family, friends, and professionals to help ease the strain that comes with fatherhood.

With these in place, new fathers are better equipped to handle the rigors of parenting and life post-birth. Supporting new fathers through understanding their physical and emotional needs should be a priority for those close to them and society.

Physical Strain on New Moms

Your wife just gave birth! Hooray! While new mothers are likely to be more aware of the physical and mental strain of caring for a newborn, many underestimate how much their lives can be affected after delivery.

And you're going to need to be there every step of the way to help support her and make the transition as painless as possible. Because trust me, she will be in a lot of pain!

New moms often find themselves in a difficult physical and mental situation once a child is born. The caregiving responsibilities of a newborn can put a significant amount of strain on new mothers, leading to fatigue, muscle aches, changes in sleep patterns, and more. The support of family and friends is essential for new moms to make the transition as comfortable as possible.

Husbands can help take some burdens off by doing what they can around the house, including grocery shopping or taking care of other errands. Additionally, pitching in with diaper changing, feeding time, and nighttime rocking can be instrumental in helping around the house.

This will benefit your wife and allow you to bond with your baby while helping your wife recover. Building this relationship early in life is fundamental to developing any healthy parent-child bond. It's important to remember that this period won't last forever - eventually, your wife will feel like herself again soon enough!

However, for now, husbands must understand the demands placed on their wives so that they can better show their love and care through actions such as providing her extra rest or breaking up household chores - both will go a long way in relieving some pressure from new moms during this hectic but wonderful time!

New mothers often find themselves in a difficult situation post-delivery. Not only is this time filled with physical pain, such as labor and postpartum recovery, but it can also be emotionally taxing.

Childbirth's hormonal and psychological impacts can take its toll on new moms, leading to fatigue, muscle aches, and disrupted sleep patterns.

Understanding the demands placed on new mothers through this period is essential for husbands to support their wives during recovery time better.

This can include doing what they can around the house to help lighten the load, like grocery shopping or taking care of other errands. Pitching in with diaper changing, feeding time, and nighttime rocking goes a long way in helping out, too.

It's important to view this period not as an inconvenience but as an opportunity for fathers to build a strong relationship with their children early on in life. This will create a lasting bond between parent and child throughout life.

New mothers need extra love and care during this hectic yet wonderful stage - providing her with extra rest or anything else she may need will help her immensely!

New mothers often find themselves deprived of sleep once a child is born. The constant demands of caring for a newborn and childbirth's physical and psychological toll can lead to extreme fatigue and exhaustion.

This can be very dangerous for both mom and baby - new moms need to ensure they get the proper rest to recharge their bodies to continue providing the best care possible.

Many underestimate just how much sleep a new mother needs to recover from the strain of childbirth and ensure their baby is safe and well-fed.

Husbands should be aware of this when helping out around the house - even if it's only taking care of simple tasks like grocery shopping or running errands, this will give her an extra opportunity to catch up on some much-needed rest.

Additionally, pitching in with diaper changing, feeding time, and nighttime rocking can help greatly reduce the burden placed on her shoulders.

Fathers should take advantage of these moments to help build a strong bond with their children early on in life. Husbands need to realize that providing new mothers with extra love and care during this trying yet wonderful time will make all the difference!

New mothers often need extra love and care during their postpartum recovery period, yet they are often not given the necessary support to make it through.

New moms face a key issue: a lack of assistance with physical tasks at home, such as shopping, cleaning, or meal preparation while recovering from labor.

Husbands should know that even grocery shopping or running errands will help lighten the load on new mothers during this time. They can also pitch in with diaper changing, feeding time, and nighttime rocking - activities that provide additional help and build strong relationships between parent and child.

Fathers need to view postpartum recovery not as an inconvenience but as an opportunity to build a lasting bond with their child early on in life. Providing new mothers with extra love and care during this difficult yet wonderful stage will help them physically and emotionally!

In today's world, it is easy for new parents to be overwhelmed by the sheer amount of information available about childcare and parenting techniques.

It can be hard to know what advice to follow and what to ignore; however, some outdated parenting practices should be avoided. One example is paying attention to modern medical advice on sleep training, feeding techniques, and vaccinations.

Co-sleeping or extended breastfeeding may have been commonplace decades ago, but research has shown that they either have little benefit or pose potential risks.

These outdated practices must not be used to ensure the safety and well-being of both parent and child. Another practice that should be avoided is setting too rigid a schedule for your newborn.

Babies often exceed expectations regarding development rates - pushing them to "set" milestones can create undue stress for both parties involved. Parents should instead focus on providing their children with the utmost love and care while allowing them to develop at their own pace.

Other outdated parenting practices for newborns include light exposure stimulation, which is exposing newborns to bright lights or loud noises to stimulate their development. This practice has been proven ineffective and can counterproductively affect a baby's development.

Another outdated parenting practice is that babies should be put on a strict sleep schedule, such as napping regularly throughout the day and having specific bedtimes at night. The truth is that newborns are still developing their circadian rhythms and often do not need a set bedtime.

It can be beneficial to allow them to nap when they want during the day, as this will help their bodies adjust more quickly to the natural cycle of day and night.

Finally, it is important to avoid the outdated belief that babies should not be allowed to cry too much or for too long. In reality, some crying is normal and healthy for newborns as it helps with emotional regulation. It's important for parents to understand that babies will cry sometimes and that it is not necessarily an indication of something being wrong - rather, it is simply a way for them to communicate needs or desires!

By avoiding outdated parenting practices and following modern medical advice, parents can better provide for their newborns while keeping both parties safe, healthy, and happy!

As a new parent, navigating the uncertain times that come with a newborn can be difficult. Not knowing where to turn for help or what resources are available can make parenting even more stressful than it already is.

Parents need to be aware of the resources available to them during this time that could help lighten their burden. For instance, parents may not be aware of social services such as food banks, clothing exchanges, and parenting classes that can provide much-needed assistance without breaking the budget.

Additionally, professional counseling and therapy services are available for those struggling with depression, anxiety, postpartum blues, or other mental health issues. Finally, financial aid from organizations like SNAP or WIC can provide families with extra support during difficult times.

By being aware of these resources and taking advantage of them when needed, parents can lessen the burden of raising a newborn and create a more positive experience for themselves and their child in this monumental life transition.

Raising a newborn can be overwhelming and stressful, but parents don't have to do it alone.

By avoiding outdated parenting practices such as extended breastfeeding or light exposure stimulation and taking advantage of resources like social services, professional counseling, and financial aid, parents can provide their children with the best care possible while supporting themselves in this monumental life transition.

Raising a newborn with the right help and support system doesn't have to feel daunting. Parenting should be an enjoyable experience - not one that leaves you feeling constantly overwhelmed!

Breast & Bottle Feeding

Breastfeeding or bottle-feeding are both valid methods of providing nutrition for newborns. While breastfeeding has been widely recognized as the most natural and beneficial way to feed a baby, bottle feeding can provide an alternative for those who cannot or choose not to breastfeed.

When selecting a feeding method, parents need to know the techniques available so they can make an informed decision about which one is best for their baby.

For example, the proper latching technique is essential for successful breastfeeding. If latching issues arise, consulting a lactation professional may help troubleshoot these problems.

Similarly, when bottle-feeding, there are various techniques to consider, such as pacing the feedings with pauses every few minutes or alternating between bottles and breastfeeding sessions if desired. In addition, selecting a high-quality bottle and nipple that work best for your baby's particular needs will ensure a comfortable experience during feeding times.

By educating themselves on the options available and finding out what works best for their baby, parents can make an informed decision about feeding their newborn.

Breastfeeding offers many benefits to both mother and baby. The proper latching technique is essential for successful breastfeeding, and by developing a good latch, mothers can ensure that their babies receive the full range of nutrients and antibodies.

In addition, breastfeeding provides optimal nutrition and strengthens the bond between mother and child. It also helps protect against certain illnesses and diseases, boost immunity, enhance development, reduce the risk of obesity, and provide an easy way to feed on the go.

Breastfeeding also helps reduce the risk of Sudden Infant Death Syndrome (SIDS) because when babies are placed on their backs to sleep, they cannot roll over and become stuck, leading to death.

Furthermore, breastfeeding is cost-effective and requires no additional equipment or storage space, making it a great option for busy parents. It does not contain added sugars or preservatives that may be found in formula-fed foods and is much easier for babies to digest. Recent studies have suggested that breastfeeding could even reduce the risk of certain cancers in both mother and child.

Bottle feeding can be a great way to ensure that mother and baby both get the rest they need. Parents may choose to alternate between breastfeeding, and bottle feeds if desired or use bottles as the primary food source for their baby.

It is important to ensure that high-quality bottles are chosen so the baby's nutrition needs are met, and choosing the right bottle and nipple for the baby's needs is key. Many moms might opt for disposable bags or pre-made formula when bottle-feeding, but some parents might choose to prepare their formula using powdered ingredients.

In addition, added probiotics in the formula can help with various digestive issues and fuel healthier immune systems. Bottle feeding should also be done in a reclined position to help reduce the chance of choking and encourage better digestion.

Making an informed decision when it comes to feeding your baby is key. It can be helpful to learn about all the options available and speaking with experienced parents, healthcare providers, and other experts in the field can help you find out what works best for your baby.

Whether you choose formula, breastfeeding, or a mix of both, knowing the pros and cons of each choice will give you a better understanding of what would work best for your family's dynamic. Taking into account any allergies or special dietary needs your baby might have may also factor into making an educated decision.

Choosing the best feeding method is an important decision that requires careful consideration. Breastfeeding and bottle-feeding offer unique benefits, but each option has certain drawbacks. It's important to research all available options to make the most informed decision possible.

By educating yourself on what works best for your baby's particular needs, you can ensure a comfortable experience during feeding while providing optimal nutrition and strengthening the bond between mother and child.

Nutrition & Feeding Schedules

Feeding your infant can be an exciting and rewarding experience, but it is important to ensure they get the nutrition they need. Ensuring your infant gets the nutrition they need is essential for healthy growth and development.

To ensure your baby is receiving proper nourishment, here are some helpful guidelines for establishing a healthy nutrition and feeding schedule: From understanding key nutrients to setting up a routine that works best for your family, getting familiar with these tips can help ensure your infant both looks and feels their best.

Starting solid foods can be an exciting milestone for your baby, although it's best to wait until they're around six months old before introducing them. Their digestive system is more developed at this stage and ready to digest semi-solid and solid foods.

Some signs that your baby may be ready for solids include sitting up unassisted, showing interest in food, and having developed the ability to move food from the front of their tongue to the back. It's important to start with soft purees or mashed foods so your baby can get used to the different textures.

Gradually introduce new flavors and textures as they become more comfortable with eating. Monitor their reaction to see if any food does not agree with them.

When introducing your baby to solid foods, it's important to introduce them one food at a time and wait a few days between introducing each new food. This is to ensure they are not reacting negatively to any particular food.

Also, always remember to feed your small infant portions of the new food as you gradually increase the amount over time. It's also useful to keep a record of foods consumed to stay on top of any allergies or reactions.

If your baby does experience an allergic reaction, contact your doctor for further advice on how best to proceed.

Once your baby reaches around six months, it is time to introduce iron-rich foods into their diet. This is important for their healthy growth and development, as iron helps carry oxygen from the lungs throughout the body.

Some good sources of iron for babies include iron-fortified cereals, red meat, lentils, beans, and tofu - make sure you cut them into small pieces to reduce the chance of choking.

When introducing these foods to your baby, it's important to remember that their digestive tract is still developing, so patience is key. Start by offering small amounts and gradually increase the quantity over several feedings.

Until your baby turns one year old, breast milk or formula should still be their main source of nutrition. Although it's important to introduce solid foods from around the six-month mark, breast milk and formula are essential for providing the key nutrients that a growing baby needs.

They contain vitamins and minerals like iron, zinc, and calcium, which are critical for their development. Up to 12 months of age, Breast milk or formula should make up most of your baby's daily diet, and regular meals should supplement this.

Feeding your baby a combination of breast milk or formula and iron-rich solid foods is essential until they reach the age of 12 months. This helps ensure they receive all the nutrients needed to grow and develop properly.

Ensuring the Best Sleep Possible

Creating a healthy sleep schedule for your newborn or infant can be invaluable in the first few months. As babies grow and develop, they'll need different amounts of sleeping time depending on their age, making it difficult to understand how much sleep is enough.

Fortunately, there are a variety of strategies that parents, caregivers, and pediatricians can all use to help establish a consistent and healthy sleep routine for babies.

From swaddling techniques and gentle rocking motions to comforting sounds and skin-to-skin contact, having the right knowledge about suitable sleeping habits may be the key to helping a baby rest easily.

Newborns have yet to establish their circadian rhythm, which is the body's natural sleep-wake cycle. As a result, newborns take short naps during the day and sleep for longer stretches at night. It is important to monitor the amount of sleep your baby gets and ensure they meet their daily requirements.

While it may seem difficult for newborns to stick to a bedtime routine, providing consistent cues like dimming lights or playing relaxing music can help them recognize when it is time for sleep. Establishing healthy sleep habits early on will help ensure your baby gets the quality rest they need.

Babies are often comforted by noise, such as white noise or soothing lullabies, which can help aid in achieving restful sleep. White noise helps to block out sudden loud noises, which could startle your baby during their slumber.

Playing a gentle melody or calming song can also help create a tranquil atmosphere and encourage restful sleep. Creating a consistent bedtime routine with these comforting sounds helps your baby recognize when it is time to drift off into dreamland.

Establishing a routine early on can help babies learn when it is time to sleep. This could include singing a song, reading stories, having a warm bath, or giving them a massage before bedtime. These calming routines will create an atmosphere of security and familiarity that will signal babies when it's time to wind down and rest.

Additionally, sticking to a consistent sleeping pattern, such as waking up at the same time each day, will signal the body when it is time to sleep and create healthy habits that will last into adulthood.

Creating a comfortable sleeping environment is important when helping your baby get the restful sleep they need. Ensure their bed or crib is well-ventilated, warm, and free of sharp edges.

Soft fabrics around them, such as plush blankets or stuffed animals, provide comfort and security that will help encourage peaceful slumber. Additionally, keeping the room dark by using curtains or tinted windows will help babies recognize when nighttime has arrived.

Infants should also be placed on their backs when sleeping to reduce the risk of Sudden Infant Death Syndrome (SIDS). Parents should ensure the baby is secured with a tight-fitting sheet or mattress that won't bunch up around them.

Furthermore, it is recommended that parents avoid putting loose bedding, pillows, and stuffed animals in the crib, as these can obstruct a baby's breathing and increase their risk for SIDS. Taking these precautions can help ensure your baby gets the restful sleep they need without putting them at risk for any potential dangers.

To further promote better sleeping habits in your baby, one should avoid stimulating activities right before bedtime, such as watching TV or playing video games, as this can affect the quality of their rest. An ideal pre-bedtime routine could involve things like reading a book or soft music, which helps to calm and relax both baby and parent just before sleep.

Keep a consistent bedtime routine so that children learn when it is time to wind down each night and recognize when to rest and relax.

To ensure a peaceful environment for your infant to sleep in, try to keep nighttime disruptions to a minimum by dimming lights and minimizing noise.

A dark, quiet place can help your little one relax and easily drift off into a peaceful sleep, and this can also aid in maintaining consistency and routine throughout their bedtime schedule.

In addition to avoiding nighttime disruptions, one should limit naps during the day so that your baby is more likely to stay asleep at night.

While it may be tempting to let your baby rest whenever possible throughout the day, one should set a schedule for daytime naps and stick with it to promote better sleeping habits overall.

Safe Sleep Practices for Babies

Adopting safe sleep practices is essential for babies to reduce the risk of Sudden Infant Death Syndrome (SIDS).

Make sure to place your baby on their back to sleep, as this has been shown to reduce the risk of SIDS. Use a firm, flat surface for sleep, and make sure that the bedding is tight-fitting and breathable. Avoid using soft objects such as pillows or stuffed animals in the crib.

Keep the baby's sleeping area free from blankets, toys, and clutter. Lastly, ensure that the baby sleeps in their own space, not with another person or pet.

Sudden Infant Death Syndrome (SIDS) is the sudden and unexplained death of an infant under one year of age, which can occur while the baby is asleep. It is the leading cause of death among babies between one month and one year old in many countries.

The exact cause of SIDS remains unknown, but it is thought to be related to a combination of factors that put an infant at higher risk, including sleeping position, temperature control, and unsafe sleep environments.

When it comes to a baby's sleeping environment, doctors and childcare experts advise that soft bedding should be avoided when putting your baby to bed.

This includes blankets, pillows, and bumper pads, which can cause suffocation. It is important that the mattress is firm and fits snugly against the crib's sides.

A sleeping baby should never be left unattended in an infant seat, swing, or carrier. Furthermore, co-sleeping with a baby should not occur if you are under the influence of drugs or alcohol or if you are a smoker.

Doctors and childcare experts recommend waiting until your baby is at least one year old before introducing pillows and blankets. This will help to reduce the risk of SIDS, as infants are more likely to suffocate due to soft bedding.

Additionally, the blanket should fit securely over the mattress so that it does not interfere with your baby's breathing. It is important to keep in mind that a sleeping baby should never be left unattended in an infant seat, swing, or carrier. When introducing pillows and blankets, ensure they are always kept away from your baby's face to prevent suffocation.

When it comes to a baby's sleeping environment, doctors and childcare experts advise that cribs and mattresses should have a firm surface to ensure optimal safety for your infant.

Ensure their mattress is firm and fits snugly against the crib's sides. Soft bedding, such as blankets, pillows, and bumper pads, should be avoided as these can cause suffocation. Additionally, a sleeping baby should never be left unattended in an infant seat, swing, or carrier, nor should they sleep with you if you are under the influence of drugs or alcohol or a smoker.

Help Your Baby Fall Asleep

Swaddling is a common practice used to provide comfort and security to young babies by mimicking the feeling of being in the womb. It involves wrapping your baby in a thin or receiving blanket so that its arms and legs are tucked in snugly.

The key to successful swaddling is to ensure that it is not too tight and that your baby's hips can move freely and naturally. In addition, make sure you only swaddle your baby while they are lying down as opposed to while they are moving or standing. Swaddling can help keep your infant calm and give them a better night's rest.

Gentle rocking can be a great way to help comfort and relax your baby to ensure a peaceful sleep. This method works best while the baby is lying in their crib, though it can also be done while they are in your arms if needed.

The motion should mimic a boat moving on gentle waves - back and forth, side to side, or a combination of both - but not too vigorous. This motion helps lull the baby and can often encourage them to go into a deep sleep quickly.

Going for a stroller walk or riding in the car can effectively soothe and calm your infant. The natural motion of walking or being in the car helps stimulate the baby's senses, often resulting in feelings of relaxation. In addition, you must make sure that your infant is properly secured for safety purposes.

If going for a walk, ensure that your stroller is well balanced so as not to tip over while walking and that your baby has plenty of room to move around even when strapped in their harness. If you plan on taking a car ride with your baby, always ensure they are securely fastened into their car seat according to manufacturer instructions.

A baby's sleep needs vary depending on age, but babies generally need at least 16 to 18 hours daily. Newborns typically sleep for up to 18 hours while they grow and develop, while babies aged 4-12 months need 14-15 hours of sleep. As babies become toddlers, they require less sleep and may only need 12-14 hours per day. Some babies may also take several naps throughout the day in addition to their nighttime sleeping schedule. Ensuring that your baby gets enough sleep is important for their physical, mental, and emotional health, so it is important to monitor the amount of rest your baby is getting each day.

Several things can be done to create a comfortable sleeping environment for your baby to get the restful sleep they need. Creating a consistent bedtime routine and keeping the noise level down in the room are two good ideas.

In addition, maintain a temperature between 65-70 degrees Fahrenheit in the room and ensure that your baby has comfortable bedding. If possible, avoid using electronic devices near where your baby sleeps, as they could interfere with their sleep quality.

Finally, you must talk to your pediatrician if you have any questions or concerns about how much sleep your baby is getting and how best to help them get the rest they need.

Overall, it is important to remember that every baby will have different needs concerning sleep and rest. However, using the strategies outlined earlier, such as swaddling, gentle rocking motions, and providing comfort through skin-to-skin contact or going for a stroller walk, can help create a healthy sleep routine for your infant.

With patience and consistency, you should be able to establish an effective sleeping schedule that works best for both you and your baby. Remember - consult your pediatrician if you are still determining how much sleep is enough or what techniques may work best for your little one!

Example Newborn Schedule

- 0-2 hours: Feeding followed by Swaddling and Sleep
- 2-4 hours: Awake time (e.g., Skin to skin contact, tummy time, talking/singing/reading stories)
- 4-6 hours: Feeding followed by Swaddling and Sleep
- 6-8 hours: Awake time (e.g., Skin to skin contact, tummy time, talking/singing/reading stories)
- 8-10 hours: Feeding followed by Swaddling and Sleep
- 10+ hours: Awake time (e.g., Skin to skin contact, tummy time, talking/singing/reading stories)

Newborns need to feed every 2-4 hours during the day and about every 3-5 hours at night. You may notice longer stretches at night starting around six weeks of age. If your baby is not waking up on their own for nighttime feedings by eight weeks, consult your pediatrician.

It is important to recognize that a newborn's sleep and wake cycles are not like an adults. Your baby will likely be awake for 1-2 hours stretches at times, then sleep for 1-3 hours at a time, often broken up by feedings throughout the day and night. As your baby ages, its sleep cycles may shift and become more regular.

Remember that all babies are different, and you should always follow your instincts when developing your baby's schedule.

Every family has unique rhythms, so trust yourself as you find the best schedule for you and your baby. Also, remember to take care of yourself -

include some rest time in your daily routine!

Changing a Diaper

Dads, changing a diaper on a newborn baby for the first time can be daunting. But do not worry; we're here to help. So, grab your supplies, and let us get started!

It would help if you first collected all the supplies you'll need - diapers, wipes, a changing pad, etc.

When preparing for a baby, there is nothing more important than ensuring you have all the supplies and gear ready. Diapers are number one on the list, as well as some wipes, a changing pad, and ointments. It can be overwhelming to pick a brand you trust, but you'll find your way soon enough!

Look into any special baby items such as pacifiers and teethers – they are not always essential, but they can make your life easier in those early years. Organizing everything beforehand will give you peace of mind and prepare your home for anything when your bundle of joy arrives!

Ensure the area where you're changing the diaper is clean - no one wants to lie down on a dirty surface!

When it's time to change a diaper, that little one needs to feel safe and secure - no one wants grime and germs on their bum! Make sure the area is clean: take a few minutes to dust the surfaces, wipe down any spills, or shake out any remaining crumbs.

If the surface is big enough, you can lay down a towel or changing mat for additional protection. Babies appreciate a clean and tidy space, and I will thank you later - no one likes a dirty diaper surprise!

Place your baby on its back on the changing pad and open up the diaper.

It's time to change your baby's diaper, a process that takes just a few steps to complete. Start by laying your baby face up on a clean changing pad, and make sure the pad is fully open and spread out for sanitary purposes.

Begin to gently remove their clothes so you can easily access their legs and waistline. Once everything is clear and ready to go, open the diaper itself —

this could require some practice if you've never done it before!

With a few moments of preparation, you'll be able to give your little one a fresh, safe diaper in no time!

Clean up any messes with the wipes and then put on a new diaper.

Caring for a baby is a lot of work, but it doesn't have to be a struggle if you know what you're doing. When it's time to change the baby's diaper, clean up any messes with the wipes and then put on a new diaper.

Disposable ones are often preferred as they are convenient and weigh less messy than cloth diapers!

You can even get special scented or non-scented wipes depending on your preference and that of the baby. After you've cleaned up and put on a fresh diaper, your little one will feel much more comfortable; look how happy they are now!

Fasten the diaper snugly but not too tight, and dispose of the old one properly.

Changing a diaper might seem tricky and intimidating, but it can be easy with a little practice and knowledge of the basics. Make sure the diaper fits snugly around your baby with room to move.

Don't fasten it too tightly, or it might cause irritation, but keep in mind that if it's not on tightly enough, accidents can happen! Once your new diaper is on, remember to throw away the dirty diaper properly, so you don't create a smelly situation for yourself.

If you have been out and about today, there is one thing you need to do as soon as possible - wash your hands thoroughly! Soap up those digits and scrub away all the icky germs that inevitably leave your venture.

Not only will this keep you safe from any illnesses you may have picked up, but it also keeps everyone else around you safe. So remember - when you come back home, make sure your hands are squeaky clean!

Safely Bathe a Newborn

Hey first-time dads, have you ever been left alone with your newborn and had no idea how to bathe them? Do not worry; we have all been there.

Bathing a newborn can be daunting, but you'll be a pro in no time. So grab a cup of coffee and settle in - it's time to learn how to bathe a baby!

Filling the tub just right can be tricky. You do not want it too hot, or you will end up overheating, but you don't want it too cold either because that defeats the whole point.

Aim for somewhere between and stay within a few inches of warm water - this is the sweet spot! If you add too much water, run a colder tap simultaneously to keep it balanced and ensure that everything stays just as it should be.

Bathing your baby for the first time can be a daunting experience! Instilling confidence and communication is key for a soothing and successful bath. Start by preparing the environment with warm, gentle water and ensure that the temperature is comfortable for them using a warm-water thermometer.

Once everything is ready, carefully pick up your little one with two hands beneath their neck, torso, and legs while supporting their head and neck; gently lower them into the bath, ensuring they remain comfortable!

Utilize physical movements to help relax your baby in the water, such as sweetly caressing their skin or singing calming lullabies — whatever it takes to make them feel secure. An enjoyable bath time awaits!

You want to keep your baby's skin healthy and clean, so when it comes to washing, less is more. Rather than harsh chemicals, use a mild, unscented soap on their body that is safe and gentle enough for their delicate skin.

Always avoid their face when using the soap - save that sensitive area for a plain warm water rinse or a very mild face wash that will not irritate.

When cleaning the rest of them up, take your time and be extra mindful of avoiding areas like those around the eyes, nose, and other sensitive spots - no one wants to walk away with an unexpected baby bubble bath!

Taking the time to rinse all the soap with clean water after using it is a really important step! Even if you think that you've gotten most of the product off your skin or your hair, some lingering residue could still be left behind.

If you don't take ten seconds to rinse it away thoroughly, it'll trap dirt or oil and irritate.

Not only that, but if you're using a bar of harsh chemical-ridden soap, not rinsing it properly can also lead to skin sensitivities. So make sure to do your due diligence and give yourself one last rinse when necessary!

After a relaxing dip in the tub, it's time to wrap your little one up and start a fun evening. Gently scoop your baby out of the tub with both hands and wrap them in a soft, cozy towel. Don't forget to dry between all those cute little toes!

Then you can place them in a warm and safe spot on the floor to dress or give them a nice massage. Enjoy every minute of this precious moment as babies grow up so fast!

After a bath, most parents will want to get their little ones dried off as quickly as possible. However, taking care of that baby's skin is very important! Babies, especially newborns, have very fragile and sensitive skin - so instead of rubbing the water off, pat their skin dry.

With just a few gentle parts, you can ensure your baby is dry without causing any irritation or redness!

Additionally, you'll want to ensure you're using soft towels to pat them, as anything too rough could be uncomfortable for them. So next time your little one needs some drying after a bath - skip the rubbing and pat them down with extra love and care.

Chapter 8

Keeping Your Newborn Safe

When it comes to newborn safety, the most important thing is understanding the risks and taking the necessary steps to protect your baby.

From ensuring they are always in a safe sleeping space to learning infant CPR and choosing the right car seat, it is essential to become informed and educated on how best to care for your precious little one.

Learning Infant CPR

Warning: This information is for educational purposes only and should NOT be considered an adequate substitute for professional training from a certified instructor by a reputable organization, such as your local hospital, fire station, or American Red Cross.

Attempting to perform infant CPR without the proper instruction and accreditation can cause injury to the infant and lead to poor outcomes.

Learning the proper technique for infant CPR is essential for caretakers who may face an emergency requiring resuscitation. Generally, the steps include tilting the head back and pinching the nostrils shut while providing two rescue breaths into the mouth.

Next, chest compressions should be done at a rate of 30 compressions per minute; to achieve this, caregivers can count out "one-and-two-and" until they reach thirty.

After every five sets of chest compressions, two more rescue breaths should be given, and then the cycle is repeated until medical help arrives or until the infant shows signs of recovery.

It is important to note that each step must be performed properly to have a successful outcome following the initiation of CPR on an infant.

Practicing proper technique on an infant mannequin or dummy can help caretakers become more comfortable performing CPR. However, it should not be considered an adequate substitute for professional instruction and certification. Taking a class from a certified instructor is the best way to learn how to properly administer CPR on an infant in an emergency.

Accident Prevention

Safety devices around the house are a great way to protect young children from accidents and avoid potentially life-threatening situations. Age-appropriate safety devices can prevent household dangers such as falls, fires, and drowning.

Parents must ensure that their home is equipped with the appropriate safety devices to protect children from these hazards. This will discuss age-appropriate safety devices around the house that can help prevent accidents and keep children safe.

Safety devices can help prevent falls around the house. Baby gates and window guards are critical equipment to help keep young children from potential fall hazards like staircases or balconies.

Child-proof locks on doors and cabinets keep curious kids away from dangerous rooms or contents. High chairs, potty chairs, booster seats, and harnesses can also ensure children stay secure while seated. Rugs and mats should be placed over slippery surfaces to reduce the risk of falls.

Fire protection devices are essential for any home. Smoke alarms should be installed around the house, near bedrooms and other living areas.

Fire extinguishers should also be easily accessible when a fire is detected.

Additionally, carbon monoxide detectors can detect dangerous gases that may otherwise go unnoticed. It's also important to ensure that all electrical wiring is up-to-date and secure against potential hazards and have fire sprinklers installed and check them regularly.

Extra care should be taken for water safety for a newborn or child up to one year of age.

Bathtubs should be equipped with anti-slip mats, and no more than two inches of water should be used in a bath. Water sources should always supervise babies as they can easily drown in small amounts.

Children under one should not wear inflatable floatation devices as these can deflate suddenly and cause them to sink.

Drain covers designed for infants are made from special materials to prevent objects from blocking the water path into sewers and causing potential harm.

Placing locks on toilet lids and bathroom doors is also an important precaution that can help protect babies from drowning accidents.

When it comes to babyproofing a home, staircases should always be at the top of the list. Installing a baby gate at the top or bottom of stairs is a great way to prevent falls and other accidents.

Open electrical sockets should also be covered with safety plugs to avoid electrocution.

Using corner and edge guards on furniture can help cushion hard edges, reduce the risk of injury from bumping into sharp edges, and installing products like door locks and window latches for doors and windows that could pose a danger if opened is essential for keeping your little one safe.

It's important to take the necessary steps to ensure a safe environment for children up to one year of age.

Installing safety products like baby gates, safety plugs, and corner or edge guards can help protect against dangerous falls, electrocution, and other hazards that can arise in the home. Taking the time to properly babyproof a home is essential for keeping babies safe.

Proper Clothing

As a dad, you must ensure your newborn is dressed properly. Babies need an extra layer of clothing compared to the amount adults wear to feel comfortable.

This extra layer of clothing helps keep your baby warm and cozy on cold days and cool on hot days.

With so many options available, it can be overwhelming to pick the right clothing for your newborn. Fortunately, a few tips and tricks can help guide you in making the best choices for your infant.

Pajamas are a great option for newborns. When picking out pajamas, look for ones with no buttons, ties, or snaps - this is important to avoid strangulation hazards.

Choose materials like cotton or fleece to keep the baby warm and comfortable. Additionally, look for footed pajamas that go over the feet and zip up the front for easy changing.

A hat is a must-have for newborns - it helps to prevent heat loss through the head. Choose one that fits snugly so it won't slip off during movement, and pick out one with a wide brim or visors for extra protection from the sun.

Many options are available in different colors and styles, so you can easily find the perfect hat to keep your baby comfortable.

When choosing clothes for your newborn, it's important to pick out breathable and comfortable materials. Natural materials like cotton, linen, or silk are all great options, as they allow air to pass through and help keep the baby cool.

Avoid synthetics such as polyester, rayon, and wool, as these tend to trap heat and moisture, leading to discomfort for your little one.

Regarding newborns and blankets, you should always look for lightweight options with a snug fit. Ensure the wrap isn't too tight, which could cause overheating or suffocation.

Look for breathable materials such as cotton, muslin, and fleece, and opt for designs with buttons or zippers that can be easily adjusted. This way, you can keep your baby warm without compromising safety.

When dressing your newborn, comfort and safety should be your top priority. Keep your little one cozy and warm with breathable materials such as cotton and muslin, and make sure their blankets fit snugly without risking overheating or suffocation. Your baby will thank you for it!

Self-Care as a Form of Newborn Safety

Focusing on yourself can make all the difference for a few minutes or hours. Find activities you enjoy, such as hobbies, reading, or exercise, that can fit into pockets of spare moments.

Even something as simple as taking a relaxing bath or meditating for 15 minutes can be immensely helpful in reducing stress and giving you something to look forward to amidst the craziness of parenting.

Make sure you are taking the time to do things that bring you joy and make you feel fulfilled. It could be anything from listening to music or going for a walk to taking an online course or learning a new skill.

Having something to look forward to in those moments of quiet can recharge your sense of motivation, so you're ready for the next hurdle parenting throws your way. With enough positivity and self-care, parenting life can be a little less chaotic and much more enjoyable!

One of the best things you can do for yourself as a parent is to take time out to focus on your needs. We all know life can be chaotic with raising children, but you must take care of your own mental and physical health while parenting.

Make sure you carve out time in your day or week to do activities that bring you joy and make you feel fulfilled. This could range from reading a favorite book, taking a yoga class, or getting enough sleep – whatever works for you!

Taking care of yourself helps reduce stress and ensures you have the energy and enthusiasm to make the most of parenthood.

One of the best things you can do for yourself as a parent is to take time out to focus on your needs. We all know life can be chaotic with raising children, but you must take care of your own mental and physical health while parenting.

Make sure you carve out time in your day or week to do activities that bring you joy and make you feel fulfilled. This could range from reading a favorite book, taking a yoga class, or getting enough sleep – whatever works for you!

Taking care of yourself helps reduce stress and ensures you have the energy and enthusiasm to make the most of parenthood.

Parenting can be daunting, and it's okay to admit that you need help. Whether it's from family, friends, or professionals, having a support system can make your life as a parent easier and less overwhelming.

Don't be afraid to ask for help when needed – this is an essential step in ensuring you have the right resources to raise your children in the best way possible. Seeking help or advice doesn't mean you are a 'bad parent' – you value your children enough to do what is best for them!

Parenthood is a lot of hard work, but it's important to make time for your relationship with your wife and other loved ones.

Finding moments for yourself when caring for children can be difficult, but spending quality time with those closest to you helps create a strong bond and promotes healthy relationships.

Take the time to nurture each other – whether going on regular date nights or simply expressing gratitude for one another – it will make a world of difference!

As you prepare for the exciting journey of parenthood, it's important to ensure you're in the right headspace. Take some time to evaluate where you're at mentally, physically, and emotionally – it will make all the difference when it comes to managing the stresses of parenting.

Investing in yourself with ample rest and activities that bring joy and relaxation will go a long way toward maintaining your well-being throughout parenthood.

Parenthood comes with tremendous joy, but it's also a challenging journey. It's important to take the time to nurture your relationship with your wife and other loved ones, as well as yourself.

Reflecting will help you maintain good mental and physical health, giving you the strength and resilience to persevere through all the ups and downs of parenthood.

Chapter 9

Creating a Nurturing Home Environment

Creating a safe and nurturing environment for our little ones is of utmost importance as new parents. From choosing furniture pieces that promote development to storing hazardous materials out of reach, there are several factors to consider when setting up a baby-friendly home.

With careful planning and consideration, we can equip our living space with elements that ensure babies have the best possible start.

Baby-Friendly Carpeting and Flooring

Creating a safe and comfortable environment for a baby can be challenging when you choose the right type of carpet or flooring. Slip-resistant materials are best for houses with babies, as they give extra traction to keep them from slipping and falling.

Also, low-pile materials, like shag carpeting, can be dangerous for babies learning to walk as they may trip over the fibers. Investing in the right carpet or flooring will help ensure your little one stays safe while exploring their new home.

Enhancing Development Through Play

Babies learn and grow mostly through play. Exploring their environment allows them to gain important physical, cognitive, and social skills that will remain with them throughout life.

When babies interact with their world, they develop a sense of trust and security, as well as help foster creativity, problem-solving skills, and hand-eye coordination. Make sure to provide your little one with plenty of opportunities for playtime to ensure they maximize their developmental potential.

Sensory Stimulation

Creating a stimulating environment for your baby can help stimulate and nurture their development. Try decorating with brightly colored walls to capture their attention or providing soft toys like stuffed animals and textured items such as rattles and blocks. These sensory objects are great for babies to explore and can allow them to learn about the world through play.

Storage Solutions

Providing your baby with the essentials they need is an important part of parenting. To ensure you have what you need regarding hygiene and comfort items, consider having ample storage solutions for diapers, wipes, and other necessities.

Investing in a few storage boxes or bins helps keep things organized and ensures you have access to items when needed. This will help save time during diaper changes and other daily routines that involve your baby.

Electrical Safety

Ensuring all electrical outlets and wires in your baby's room are covered is a must for ensuring the safety of your little one. Make sure to use outlet covers designed for babies, as regular outlet plugs can easily be removed.

Also, be aware of any exposed wiring inside the walls, as well as any extension cords that may be in the room. Taking the necessary steps to prevent easy access to these items will lessen potential danger for your child.

Baby Proof Space

Creating a safe and comfortable environment for your little one should be a top priority. Babyproofing the room is essential to ensure furniture and cabinets are secured and free from sharp edges or objects that can be easily pulled down.

Potential hazards such as small toys or trinkets should be kept out of reach, while locks and curtains should be installed on all windows, especially if the room faces a traffic area.

Through these steps, parents can provide their children with a safe space to explore and grow within limits, allowing them to gain confidence in themselves and develop emotional and social skills.

Babyproofing the room or space is paramount, as it ensures that all surfaces are non-toxic and free from objects that can easily be pulled down or cause harm.

Additionally, providing mats, cushions, and blankets gives them a soft surface to crawl around without fear of injury. Through this process, parents can have peace of mind knowing their little ones are safe while they explore and grow within limits.

Providing areas where babies can engage in activities with minimal adult supervision is important for their development. This could involve setting up basic toys like blocks, rattles, and other small objects they can safely interact with while being monitored by an adult.

Doing this allows children to explore and learn new skills without feeling restricted, and it also allows them to gain confidence in themselves through play and the expression of emotions. Giving babies a safe and comfortable space to do so is essential for their growth and well-being.

Giving babies opportunities to practice their gross motor skills, such as crawling, walking, and climbing, is essential for their growth and development.

Having equipment such as slides, swings, climbers, and other objects readily available in a safe environment allows them to explore and learn new skills without fear of injury.

Offering different levels of challenge within the environment is important for babies' development. By providing puzzles with simple pieces or colored shapes, children can use their fine motor skills to manipulate and learn from them.

This can help babies understand problem-solving and abstract thinking while also giving them a sense of accomplishment as they develop their cognitive skills.

Not only does this enhance their physical growth, but it also helps lay a foundation for higher-level thinking processes in the future.

Chapter 10

The First 12 Months

Being a new parent is a daunting yet thrilling experience full of joy and challenges. From sleepless nights to nappy changes, the first 12 months of parenthood can be overwhelming and filled with beautiful memories everyone should cherish and celebrate.

Both parents need to take the time to prepare themselves mentally, physically, and emotionally for this exciting journey, to give themselves the strength and resilience to persevere through even the toughest times ahead.

Month One

As a new dad, your first month is full of excitement as you adjust to life as a parent and get to know your newborn baby.

The first month of being a dad is often overwhelming and exhausting, yet also filled with joy and excitement. You get to meet your baby for the first time, marvel at every little thing they do, and witness the incredible bond between them and their mother.

As you adjust to this new life as a parent, you may learn how to change diapers, calm an upset baby in the middle of the night, and spend-time bonding with your newborn.

Every moment is magical and full of discovery for you and your child. By the end of this month, you'll have done more for your child than you ever thought possible and will feel proud of what you have achieved together.

Month Two

Your second month brings more milestones, such as solid foods, rolling over, and beginning physical development.

During month two, your baby's physical development continues incredibly. You may witness them rolling over, taking their first steps, and developing their motor skills – all while exploring their environment through sight, sound, and touch.

As your baby progresses into their third month, you will begin to see even more rapid developments in its physical abilities. They can now lift their head and chest off the ground when lying on their stomach, and they may also be able to sit unsupported for brief periods.

This is also a great time to introduce new activities, such as tummy time and games that involve rolling balls back and forth with them.

Always encourage while your baby is learning these new movements and milestones, as it will help build confidence, curiosity, and security. Overall, the second month is full of exciting new milestones that inspire and surprise you.

Month Three

By three months, your baby will be much more active and alert, likely smiling and cooing in response to your affectionate gestures.

Your child will be much more active and alert by three months old. You may witness them smiling and cooing in response to your affectionate gestures and start to recognize you when you enter the room.

They may also respond positively when played with or cuddled, showing how much they appreciate your dedication as a parent.

During this month, your baby's personality will continue to shine through as they discover the world around them. It's an amazing time of growth and development for you and your little one!

This is also when your baby will begin to establish a regular sleeping pattern. They may start to sleep for longer stretches at night and take regular naps throughout the day.

This is beneficial for them and can help you as a parent to establish consistency in their daily schedule and routines - like diaper changes, meals, and playtime - which will help give them structure.

It's important to remain patient while your baby settles into this new routine and adapts to their ever-changing environment. With consistent guidance from you, they will soon be sleeping soundly and happily each night.

Month Four

During month four, your baby's curiosity and exploration of the world around them will grow even further. As they become more mobile, you may witness them starting to crawl or walk – depending on their development level.

They will discover new objects with every move, make new connections, and learn about the world around them as quickly as ever. It's a magical time for both parent and child, full of wonderment and exploration!

At this age, you may also notice that your child is beginning to show signs of strange anxiety as they become more aware of the people around them.

You will likely see them clinging to you or displaying distress when anyone else is near. This is normal and a sign they are developing a sense of security in their bond with you.

It's important to validate these feelings and spend plenty of time with each other outdoors and indoors, so they can grow familiar with the environment around them and become confident in facing new people and situations.

Month Five

By five months old, your baby will start to show signs of independent play, and their reactions to environmental stimuli will get quicker. This is also typically when babies start teething, so be prepared for a lot of drool!

They may also become more vocal with babbling and begin to utter simple words like 'mama' or 'dada' – communicating their wants and needs in a whole new way. It's an exciting time of growing independence and exploring the world around them.

Five months old is an exciting time for babies - they are busy developing their gross motor skills, and you may even notice them starting to roll over or sit up on their own. They may also be more vocal with coos and babble, focusing on simple words like 'mama' or 'dada.'

If your little one has started teething, you'll likely see a lot of drooling, along with the occasional teething toys or rings to help soothe the gums!

As they explore their environment, remember to capture these moments in photos as they grow and develop into independent children.

Month Six

During month six, your baby's cognitive milestones will take off. They may start to develop language skills, and their recall capabilities will become stronger as they can remember things for longer periods.

This is an amazing period of growth for any child, so cherish this special time in your baby's life as it passes quickly.

As your baby moves towards the end of their sixth month, you will notice how quickly they develop. Facial expressions and hand gestures will start to strengthen, as well as their motor skills.

They will become more adept at reaching out for objects and holding onto them with better grip strength.

Their reaction time will improve as they become more aware of their surroundings and actively explore. This is also a great time to introduce new textured foods into their diet, such as mashed potatoes or pureed fruits and vegetables.

Month Seven

Your baby's physical development will be in full swing by seven months! They should now be able to crawl, and some even begin to take their first steps. Keep a closer eye on them as they become more mobile – they'll be curious about everything around them. This is also a great time for introducing toys to help with their cognitive development, such as stackers or puzzles.

Babies at seven to nine months old start exploring the world around them with newfound confidence. You may find yourself encouraged and even following your baby as they crawl or begin taking its first steps!

During this time, it's important to provide your baby with stimulating activities to continue their cognitive development. This could include providing toys that your little one can explore, such as blocks or colored balls.

You can also help them practice basic skills like grabbing objects or reaching for items. These moments of exploration and learning should be treasured – capture those smiles and giggles in photos, as they won't last forever!

Month Eight

By eight months, your baby will show impressive physical development! They should now be able to sit up and crawl with confidence. Not only that, but they may even start to stand without help and attempt a few steps here and there.

This is also the perfect time to introduce them to more interactive toys like music boxes or shape sorters.

These toys can boost their cognitive development while encouraging them to explore their environment with curiosity. Remember to take lots of pictures – those moments won't only last.

Babies also begin to understand and recognize simple words and gestures by eight months old. This is a great opportunity for you to start teaching your little one basic words, such as "no" or "yes," as well as simple commands, like "come here" or "stop." This can help to develop those crucial language skills.

Additionally, it's important to encourage your baby to interact with other children and adults - even if that means playing from a distance due to social distancing rules. Providing gentle guidance during playtime can help build those vital social skills!

Month Nine

By nine months old, your baby's development is starting to speed up! By now, they should be able to crawl confidently and even attempt those first steps - although don't worry too much if that isn't the case.

In terms of language, they pick up words and phrases faster than before. This is an incredibly exciting time as your baby discovers their voice and starts to express themselves in more meaningful ways.

It's also a great opportunity to introduce new activities such as drawing or painting, playing with clay, or even reading simple books together. The options are almost endless!

Movement is also an important milestone during this stage, as your little one starts to explore the world around them. This could be anything from crawling around the house, pulling up on furniture, or even beginning to walk.

In addition to providing physical stimulation, movement can help stimulate brain development too!

Try taking your baby outdoors for walks or playing catch with a softball in the living room - both activities will help to keep them active while building strong muscles and healthy bones. With plenty of opportunities for exploration and growth at this stage, there is no better time to get creative!

Month Ten

By the tenth month, you'll be amazed at how quickly your baby's development has progressed. Their coordination skills should show now, allowing them to perform tasks like picking up small objects with a pincer grip or eating finger foods.

This is also a great time for your little ones to develop their problem-solving skills - give them simple puzzles or building blocks and watch as they figure out how to put them together.

You may even find that they can recognize certain words and begin repeating them back when spoken. This is an incredibly exciting time for both you and your baby!

By the tenth month, your baby will develop different motor skills, opening many more exploration opportunities. They may now be able to crawl more confidently and even attempt climbing when appropriate.

You may have to keep a closer eye on them - as their curiosity grows, so does the potential for mischief! As always, provide plenty of safe, stimulating activities that can help hone their newly honed coordination skills.

From sorting toys into boxes to stacking cups and beyond, there are endless possibilities at this stage to help foster their creativity and learning.

Month Eleven

By month eleven, your little one should be firmly established in their walking skills, and you may find them venturing further than before. Their blossoming sense of independence means they can now explore more without you being there to lead the way.

As much as possible, allow them to wander around in a safe area to discover new places and objects. And if you are going on outings together, make sure to bring along some toys for your little one, so they have something to focus on and explore their newfound freedom.

Your baby should be developing verbal and nonverbal communication skills by this point.

Verbal milestones can include saying simple words like "Mama" or "Dada" or repeating sounds they hear throughout the day. Nonverbal communication may look like pointing and waving in response to hearing their name.

You'll likely notice a slight preference for what your baby wants, such as a favorite toy or snack.

This is a great indication that their problem-solving capabilities are growing rapidly, and they are interested in exploring the world around them!

Month Twelve

Month twelve brings with it many exciting milestones! Your little one is officially a toddler and will do many new things daily. The primary developmental focus at this stage is language: you'll notice your child speaking in full sentences, learning new words, and repeating what they hear. They may also use simple phrases such as "please" and "thank you." Many children this age is starting to engage in pretend play, which is an important part of their development.

You may also see them exploring the boundaries of independence by pushing against rules or testing out newly-acquired physical skills like climbing stairs or running faster.

Please encourage them to explore their world but keep a close eye on them so that you can provide loving guidance with any safety concerns.

Motor control and coordination will also be a key part of your child's development during month twelve. If they have not still don't need to, they may start walking without your assistance.

This is typically the first time in their life that they can access objects or locations on their own, so you may find them suddenly curious about everything around them!

In addition to walking, most children at this age will be able to throw objects more accurately, kick a ball in some direction, and easily pick up small objects. As always, be sure to provide any necessary guidance for safety should anything get too wild or out of control!

You have now made it through your baby's first year of development. This is an incredible time for you and your little one as they continue exploring the world around them.

From verbal communication skills to physical coordination, month twelve brings a wealth of opportunities that can help shape their future learning capabilities.

With each new milestone achieved, there will be plenty of joys and challenges along the way. So make sure to enjoy every moment (even when things get wild) and celebrate all their accomplishments, no matter how big or small - this is only the beginning!

Chapter 11

The Importance of Bonding with Baby

Bonding with newborns can be one of the most meaningful experiences for new parents. Connecting on a deeper level with your baby not only creates strong emotional ties between you and your child but can also provide important developmental benefits for them.

Parents can explore different approaches to bonding with newborns to create stronger relationships and encourage healthy physical, social, and cognitive development in their babies.

Take Part in Special Bonding Activities

One way to strengthen the bond between you and your little one is to engage in activities together.

Spending quality time doing something enjoyable can help parents form a lasting connection with their baby. From reading stories, playing music, or engaging in interactive activities like baby yoga or swimming, there are plenty of ways to take part in special bonding moments.

Taking your child for a walk, visiting the library, or attending playgroups are all great opportunities for fun and connection. Going out and exploring the world encourages learning and creates long-lasting memories that you and your child will cherish forever!

Bonding with an infant can be done in many different ways, but it takes more effort than engaging with an older child. For dads, spending time reading to their little ones or playing music can help create a special bond. Rock-a-byes, singing lullabies or making funny faces are also great activities.

Placing the baby on your chest and taking a nap together is another way that dads can deeply connect and relax with their new bundle of joy.

Going for walks or taking part in simple exercises like stretching and massages can help you bond and provide beneficial exercise for your baby's development.

Spending quality time with your newborn is essential in building a strong relationship and creating lasting memories.

When parents actively invest time in creating special moments with their little ones, it helps them understand and appreciate the preciousness of the early stages of development.

It also encourages acknowledgment of growth and development, which can be easily forgotten as time passes by.

This is especially true with small children, who grow fast and may soon outgrow activities that help build a connection between parent and baby. With this fleeting nature of infancy, spending time with your newborn is truly the one thing you cannot get back.

As new dads, investing quality time with your newborn is essential. Sharing special moments creates lasting memories and builds a strong connection that will last your child's lifetime.

From exploring the outdoors to cooking meals together, there are numerous ways to create lasting experiences you can't get back. While balancing work and family life can be challenging, taking advantage of the quality time you have when away from work is invaluable - so don't miss a beat!

Physical Bonding

Physical bonding is an important part of connecting with newborns. One of the most important ways to do this is through skin-to-skin contact, which can help regulate a baby's temperature and heart rate and provide comfort.

Other approaches to physical bonding include rocking and soothing movements, massage, and bathing together. All these activities can be calming for both parent and baby and create an intimate bond between them.

Eye contact is an incredibly important part of bonding with a newborn. Staring into each other's eyes can help foster a sense of connection and security throughout the baby's life.

It's also a great way for parents to pick up on the nonverbal cues given by their infant, especially those related to their emotional needs.

Whether during a game, while exploring new objects, or simply spending time together, looking into each other's eyes can create a strong bond between parent and child.

Social Bonding

Social bonding is another important part of developing a strong connection with newborns. Babies use eye contact and body language to communicate and bond with their parents, and parents can use their body language and facial expressions to create a deeper connection.

For example, smiling at your baby, making eye contact while speaking or singing, cuddling them close, and using gentle touch helps babies feel loved and supported. In response, babies often have positive reactions, such as cooking or giggling.

Extending senses beyond sight is a key part of bonding with a newborn. Talking or singing softly to the baby, even in a quiet environment, can help them recognize different tones and emotions.

Facial expressions and gestures such as pointing, waving, and clapping are also great communication tools for parents.

These methods can help create an emotional connection between parent and child that will last for years.

Rocking the baby in your arms or playing "peek-a-boo" can be fun for parent and child alike and can also help deepen the connection through playtime. It's important to remember that bonding doesn't have to stop once the baby grows older; these activities can still be enjoyed well into childhood.

Cognitive Bonding

Playing interactive games together is a great way to bond with a baby. Introducing new objects or activities for them to explore and discover can help stimulate their curiosity and provide opportunities for connection.

Reading aloud helps babies learn the rhythm of language and familiarize themselves with different sounds, while singing songs can be soothing. These activities allow parents to connect with their newborns in meaningful ways, helping to create strong bonds that will last a lifetime.

Bonding with newborns is essential for creating strong emotional ties and promoting healthy physical, social, and cognitive development. Parents can build an intimate connection with their baby through physical bonding activities such as skin-to-skin contact or massage.

Social bonding through eye contact and body language helps create a sense of trust between parent and child. And finally, playing interactive games together provides opportunities to connect while stimulating the baby's curiosity.

All these approaches are important components of building long-lasting relationships that will benefit your little one throughout their life.

Why It is Important Early On

Creating a bond with your baby is important for their physical, emotional, and social development. As a parent, it's up to you to help nurture that connection from the beginning. Bonding with your newborn early can help create a secure and loving relationship.

A bond of trust between parent and child is essential for a child to feel safe, secure, and loved. It helps them understand that their needs will be met, that they can depend on their parents, and that they are valued.

Establishing trust early on can make all the difference in developing a trusting relationship with your baby that lasts well into adulthood.

Creating a strong emotional bond between parent and baby encourages the development of healthy self-esteem. This helps your child feel confident in their worth and capabilities and value their emotions as they grow. When a baby has secure emotional ties with its parent, it can develop into an adult who trusts its judgment and makes decisions based on what is best for them.

Parent-child connection is key when it comes to fostering effective communication. Once your child reaches the toddler stage, clear and effective communication is important for them to express their wants and needs.

Establishing a strong bond between parent and child helps ensure that both parties can communicate effectively, allowing for better understanding and responding positively.

Creating strong emotional bonds with your baby can provide them with comfort and security, even during times of stress or discomfort.

This helps instill confidence in young children, allowing them to make decisions based on their feelings and knowing what is best for them. Bonding with your baby helps build trust, the foundation for strong and meaningful relationships as they grow older.

Forming a strong connection between parents and children can also help to reduce separation anxiety. Babies and toddlers will learn to trust that their parents will come back, allowing them to be more relaxed when their parents leave the house.

This is beneficial for both parent and child, as it helps to create an atmosphere of peace and calm, encouraging healthy emotional development in your child.

Parents can help reduce their newborn's separation anxiety by creating a close bond with them. This can be done by providing a safe and nurturing environment and engaging in activities such as soothing touches, cuddling, singing, and talking.

These positive interactions will allow the baby to feel secure and loved even when their parents are away. Additionally, parents should maintain consistency in their caregiving routines to help lessen any anxiety or distress the child may experience due to separations.

Chapter 12

Tummy Time

Welcome to Tummy Time! Tummy Time is an important part of a baby's physical development, as it helps to strengthen the baby's muscles and increase balance.

It is a great way for babies to explore their environment and interact with objects. This will advise parents on how to introduce tummy time, its many benefits, and tips on making it more enjoyable.

Tummy time is a special activity designed to help babies develop physically. It involves placing babies on their tummies for a few minutes daily.

This helps strengthen the baby's core muscles, increasing balance and coordination. It also provides exciting opportunities, allowing babies to explore objects in the environment with their hands and eyes.

Ultimately, tummy time helps babies develop the physical skills they need to progress through milestones such as sitting up, crawling, and walking.

Introducing tummy time to a baby's routine has many potential benefits. These include:

- Building strength in the baby's back, neck, and shoulder muscles.
- Improved coordination and balance.
- Provide exciting exploration opportunities for babies to experience objects in their environment.
- Increased awareness of the body and its capabilities.

· Encouraging healthy sleeping habits by helping babies to stay awake longer during the day.

It is recommended that tummy time should begin when the baby is around two months old. During this early stage, supervised tummy time sessions should be done for a few minutes and gradually increase as the baby becomes more comfortable and strong.

As the baby grows, the number of tummy time sessions can also increase in duration (up to 10 minutes) or frequency (up to 3 times each day).

It is important to start tummy time slowly and ensure the baby is comfortable. A baby should always be supervised during tummy time by the parent or caregiver to ensure their safety.

During these sessions, parents should encourage their babies to lift their heads and chin off the ground to strengthen their neck muscles.

Toys can also be introduced into tummy time to draw the baby's attention toward different objects and promote further exploration. As the baby ages, it will also begin to learn how to move around on its stomach, which can help with crawling development.

Parents should continue encouraging tummy time as it has many benefits for a growing child.

Here are a few tips to help introduce tummy time and maintain safety and comfort for your newborn:

· Make sure the space you are using is free of any objects that could cause harm to your baby.
· Use interesting and colorful toys to draw their attention while on their tummies.
· Encourage your baby to lift their head and chin off the ground gradually over time instead of pushing them too hard.
· Always supervise your child during tummy time, either by you or another caregiver.
· Start slow and gradually increase the length of tummy time over time.

With patience and encouragement from mom or dad, your baby will soon take those all-important first steps!

Tummy time is an important part of a baby's development and helps build strength in the neck, back, and arms. To ensure safety and comfort during tummy time, these tips can help keep your baby comfortable while on their tummy.

- Please make sure the surface they are playing on is soft, flat, and large enough for them to move freely.
- Raise the head of the bed or mattress slightly so it's easier for your baby to lift their chin.
- Place a mirror in front of them so they can see themselves. This helps make tummy time more enjoyable and educational.
- Use interesting and colorful toys that they can safely move around with.
- Encourage your baby to lift their head and chin off the ground gradually over time instead of pushing them too hard.

Crawling

Watching your baby slowly become more and more mobile is an incredible feeling! As they take their first tentative steps toward mobility, it's important to help them learn new skills, such as crawling.

Crawling develops essential coordination, balance, and muscle strength for walking, stimulates their senses, and boosts overall confidence. With these simple tips, you can ensure your little one gets the most from this exciting stage of development.

Crawling is an integral part of a baby's development, as it helps them to become mobile and promotes physical growth. Crawling teaches babies spatial awareness and coordination and provides opportunities for sensory exploration.

It also creates a safe way for infants to move around and explore their environment, leading to increased cognitive development.

Crawling is important for strengthening the core muscles for walking and other complex motor skills. Additionally, learning how to crawl aids in developing balance and hand-eye coordination.

Crawling has many potential benefits for newborns, including:

- Improved physical development, as it helps to strengthen core muscles and promote coordination.
- An increased sensory exploration of their environment.
- A safe way to explore and move around, promoting increased cognitive development.
- Strengthening hand-eye coordination which is necessary for more complex motor skills.
- Improved balance because of crawling.

To get started with crawling development for newborns, it is important to provide a safe space for them to explore and practice. Some strategies parents might use to help their baby learn to crawl include:

- Making sure the floor is covered with clean, soft mats or blankets.
- You are providing toys or objects within reach of your baby and encouraging them to reach out and grab them.
- Ensuring there are no dangerous objects in their environment, such as on the edges of furniture or exposed wires.
- They held babies upright, supporting the back and shoulders by placing one hand behind the head and one low on their back.
- They repeatedly place your hands slightly away from their stomach, encouraging them to move towards you while they learn how to crawl.

Generally, newborns will start crawling between 6 and 10 months. At this age, babies are equipped with the necessary physical developmental milestones to begin crawling. Signs that your baby is ready to start crawling include:

- They can hold their head up for extended periods.
- They can push up onto their hands and knees while supporting most of

their weight.

- They begin to rock back and forth on all fours.
- They seem interested in moving around and exploring furniture or other objects in the room.

Here are some tips for introducing crawling to newborns:

- Provide plenty of space and a safe environment for your baby to practice.
- Place toys and objects your baby can reach to encourage them to move towards them.
- Take time each day to provide gentle touches and stimulation on the back and shoulders to help support motor skills development.
- Allow your baby to explore the environment around them at their own pace without forcing it.
- Encourage movement by clapping or singing songs as babies learn to crawl.

When introducing crawling to your newborn, keeping their safety and comfort in mind is important.

- Keep eyeing your baby as they explore, providing safe boundaries.
- Place pillows or soft surfaces around the area where you encourage your baby to crawl.
- Make sure any objects your baby may be tempted to grab are rounded and won't present a choking hazard.
- Provide plenty of positive reinforcement when your baby meets their mini-milestones, such as pushing themselves onto all fours or taking a few steps forwards.

Ensuring a safe environment is key when introducing crawling to your newborn.

- Keep objects that could present a choking hazard, such as buttons or string, out of reach.

· Place covers over any electrical outlets.
· Remove sharp edges from furniture or toys that could harm your baby.
· Provide plenty of supervision and space when your baby is practicing their crawling skills.

It is important to keep your baby comfortable while on their hands and knees in introducing crawling.

· Place soft surfaces or mats under any area where you're encouraging your baby to crawl.
· Make sure your baby has room to move freely on the floor, free from obstacles or furniture that could cause them to trip or fall.
· Give your baby plenty of breaks between practice sessions and provide a distraction like a toy or a book while taking a break.
· Provide plenty of positive reinforcement during their practice times, praising their progress and giving them hugs when they reach their mini milestones.

Introducing crawling to your newborn is an important part of their development and can be a fun experience for both parents and babies.

Standing

The transition from crawling to standing is another important milestone in a baby's development. After mastering crawling, the baby will start to explore ways to stand up and support their weight.

As the baby's leg muscles get stronger, they may start to pull themselves up to a standing position using nearby furniture, walls, or other objects. This is commonly referred to as "cruising" because the baby will use their hands to move from one object to another while standing.

At first, the baby may need to use both hands to support themselves while standing, but with practice and increased strength, they will be able to stand independently. This is a significant achievement, as it shows that the baby has gained the strength and balance to support their own body weight.

During this transition, the baby's coordination will continue to improve as they learn to balance on their own. They will also start to develop more advanced motor skills, such as walking, running, and jumping. The transition from crawling to standing is an exciting time for both the baby and their parents, as it opens up new opportunities for exploration and independence.

To support the baby's development during this transition, parents can provide safe opportunities for their baby to practice standing and walking.

This can include creating a safe, uncluttered environment, providing sturdy furniture for the baby to hold onto, and encouraging the baby to take steps between objects or towards a caregiver.

It's important to remember that every baby develops at their own pace, and some may take longer than others to make the transition from crawling to standing.

With patience, practice, and encouragement, most babies will eventually master this important milestone and continue on to other physical achievements.

Walking

Introducing walking to your newborn can help them develop coordination and balance while encouraging physical development. Place a cushion or blanket under your baby's feet while they stand up - this provides extra support and cushioning.

Please ensure there are plenty of toys or obstacles nearby that they can interact with while standing, such as a stack of books or blocks. Provide plenty of support and encouragement if your baby needs it, but don't push them too hard.

Identify any potential environmental risks that could pose a danger, such as exposed wires or slippery surfaces.

Walking is an important milestone for newborns, as it helps them develop many essential skills during their early years. Walking can help strengthen a baby's leg and core muscles, which are key for physical development.

It can also help balance and coordination, which are vital to safe mobility. Through walking, babies learn basic motor skills like turning and stopping, which will be needed when they start crawling, running, or climbing. Finally, walking provides an opportunity for socialization and interaction as babies explore their environment and interact with others around them.

To introduce walking to your newborn, start by placing a cushion or blanket under their feet while they stand up. This provides support and cushioning for their feet. It would help if you placed some toys nearby that they can interact with while standing.

Ensure the area is free from potential risks such as exposed wires or slippery surfaces. Once you have ensured the environment's safety, provide encouragement and support to your baby during their practice sessions.

Give plenty of positive reinforcement and praise when they reach milestones like standing up on their own or taking a few steps. Remember to give them breaks in between sessions and let them explore different activities like reading or playing with a toy.

Newborns typically start walking between the ages of nine and twelve months. However, this can vary from child to child; some babies may walk as early as six months old. As newborns develop more strength in their legs and feet, you may notice signs such as pulling up on furniture or standing for short periods.

As these developments occur, you should slowly introduce them to the concept of walking by providing support and encouragement. Reducing them to practice will help them eventually take their first steps independently.

- Start by placing a cushion or blanket under their feet while they stand up to provide extra support and cushioning for their feet.
- Place some toys nearby that your baby can interact with while standing.
- Provide plenty of positive reinforcement and praise when they reach milestones like standing up or taking a few steps.
- Give them breaks between practice sessions and explore activities like reading or playing with a toy.

· Slowly reintroduce the concept of walking, providing support and encouragement along the way.

Parenting Styles

There are several different parenting styles that are commonly recognized and studied by researchers.

These styles are based on how parents interact with their children and the approaches they take to discipline, communication, and other aspects of parenting. Here are some of the most common parenting styles:

There are four main parenting styles: authoritarian, authoritative, permissive, and uninvolved.

Authoritative parenting is generally the most balanced style, allowing children to express themselves while maintaining boundaries and expectations.

High expectations and strict rules with little room for negotiation or explanation characterize authoritarian parenting. Parents usually focus on setting boundaries and enforcing consequences while paying less attention to the emotional development of their children.

Conversely, authoritative parenting focuses on an equal balance between setting limits and expectations while allowing children to express themselves freely. This parenting style encourages open communication between parent and child and is generally the most accepted form of parenting.

Permissive parenting prioritizes the child's happiness over structure and consistency without much emphasis on rules or discipline. Parents are more likely to avoid confrontation in favor of providing unconditional love, even if it means overlooking certain behaviors or missteps.

Uninvolved parenting typically involves minimal investment in a child's development with an overall lack of communication and guidance. Parents may not show any interest in their children's activities or problems and may set few, if any, rules or guidelines for them to follow.

It's important to note that these parenting styles are not set in stone and may vary depending on the situation or the child's age and needs. Additionally, there is no one "right" parenting style that works for every family. Each style has its strengths and weaknesses, and what works for one child may not work for another. Ultimately, the goal of parenting is to provide love, support, and guidance to help children grow into happy, healthy, and responsible adults.

Fights or Disagreements Will Happen

Though parenting styles can vary from family to family, it's important to remember that disagreements between parents are normal and should be expected.

If a disagreement arises, it is important to discuss the issues respectfully and with some understanding. Find ways to compromise and come up with solutions so that your child's best interests are always a top priority.

Parenting can be a challenging and rewarding experience, and it's normal for disagreements to arise between parents. These conflicts can arise from differences in parenting styles, values, or expectations for their children.

While these disagreements can be frustrating and stressful, they can also be an opportunity to strengthen the communication and relationship between parents.

Approaching conflicts in parenting with respect and understanding for each other's perspectives is crucial for maintaining a healthy and productive relationship between parents.

Active listening is one of the most important skills to develop when trying to understand each other's viewpoints.

This means paying full attention to what the other person is saying, asking clarifying questions, and summarizing the key points to ensure that you understand them correctly.

When considering each other's viewpoints, it's essential to remember that everyone has their own values, experiences, and beliefs that shape their parenting style.

By taking the time to understand where the other person is coming from, you can better appreciate their perspective and work towards a solution that meets everyone's needs.

Compromise is often necessary in resolving conflicts, and finding common ground is critical for effective parenting. This means being willing to give a little to reach a mutually beneficial solution. This does not mean sacrificing your core values, but rather finding a middle ground that meets everyone's needs.

Remember that the ultimate goal in parenting is to prioritize your child's best interests. While it's natural for parents to have different opinions and approaches, it's essential to put your child's needs first.

This can mean setting aside your own preferences and working towards a solution that benefits your child.

It's also crucial to remember that parenting is a learning process, and making mistakes is inevitable. Acknowledge your faults and be willing to adjust your style if necessary.

Be patient and understanding with yourself and your partner as you navigate this new role, and don't be afraid to seek support from friends, family, or professionals.

If you and your partner have vastly different parenting styles, seeking the advice of a therapist or counselor can be a helpful way to navigate those differences.

A therapist can provide a neutral and safe space to discuss your concerns and explore the underlying issues that may be contributing to your disagreements.

Therapy can also help you and your partner gain a better understanding of each other's parenting styles, which can lead to greater empathy and appreciation.

With the guidance of a therapist, you can develop strategies to work together and find common ground, even if you have different parenting styles.

A therapist may use a variety of techniques to help you and your partner develop a shared parenting style. These may include exploring the beliefs and values that underpin your parenting approach, identifying areas of compromise, and setting clear boundaries and expectations.

A therapist may also teach communication skills to help you and your partner express your needs and concerns in a way that fosters understanding and respect.

In some cases, therapy may reveal deeper issues that are contributing to your parenting conflicts, such as unresolved personal issues or differences in values that go beyond parenting.

A therapist can help you and your partner address these underlying issues and find ways to work through them.

Seeking the advice of a therapist or counselor can be a valuable way to address parenting conflicts when you and your partner have vastly different parenting styles.

With the guidance of a therapist, you can gain a better understanding of each other's perspectives, develop strategies to work together, and find common ground that benefits your child.

Therapy can also help you and your partner address underlying issues that may be contributing to your disagreements and build a stronger, more productive relationship.

Fights or disagreements will happen in parenting, and it's essential to approach them with respect, understanding, and a willingness to compromise.

Effective communication, a focus on your child's best interests, and a willingness to learn and grow will help you develop a parenting style that works best for your family.

Chapter 13

Why Postpartum Care Is Not Just For Moms

When we think of postpartum care, we often think of the mother. But what about the father? While it's true that childbirth can take a physical and emotional toll on the mother, it's important to recognize that the father also experiences significant changes during this period. As a new dad himself, Jack Ink knows this all too well.

After the birth of my son, I experienced a range of emotions: joy, excitement, fear, and overwhelm. I was there to support my partner during the challenging postpartum phase but I also realized I needed to take care of myself. This realization can be difficult for men, who often face societal pressure and assumptions that they must be "tough" and focus solely on their partner and baby, neglecting their needs.

But neglecting your postpartum care can have ripple effects on your family's well-being. As a new father, you must be healthy and supported to be your best partner and parent. Prioritizing your well-being is not only good for you—it's good for your entire family.

So, how can new fathers prioritize their postpartum care?

1. Recognize childbirth's physical and emotional toll: Childbirth can also be a challenging and transformative experience for fathers. Acknowledging and processing your emotions and caring for your physical health is important. This can include exercise, good nutrition, and rest within

the limitations of your situation.

2. Ask for help when needed: Raising a child is a team effort, and asking for help is okay. This can include asking family members or friends for support or seeking professional help.

3. Find ways to connect with your partner: Communicate with your partner about your feelings, and connect beyond the baby. Setting aside time to spend together can help strengthen your relationship and support your mental health.

4. Take care of your mental health: Postpartum depression is not exclusive to mothers. New fathers can also experience symptoms of anxiety and depression during this period. It's essential to recognize the warning signs and seek help if needed.

Prioritizing your postpartum care can positively impact the entire family. By taking care of yourself, you are better equipped to care for your partner and child and model self-care and emotional literacy for them.

In actuality, postpartum care is not just for mothers - new dads also play a crucial role in the postpartum period. It's an opportunity to grow and learn as a partner and parent. So, as a new father, prioritize your postpartum care and be proud of it. Your family will thank you for it.

The postpartum period is critical for new mothers, but it is also a time of great change and adjustment for fathers. Historically, fathers have been left out of the conversation around postpartum care. Still, the reality is that dads' involvement in this matter is crucial for the well-being of both parents and their newborns.

Studies have shown that fathers in postpartum care have better emotional and physical outcomes. A father's involvement has been linked to a decreased risk of postpartum depression for mothers, leading to better bonding between the father and child. Furthermore, research has found that babies whose fathers are actively involved in their care have better cognitive and developmental outcomes.

Many fathers have seen the effects of their involvement firsthand. Brad, a father of a two-month-old, remembers feeling unsure of how to help his partner during the first few weeks post-birth, but as he became more involved in caring for their baby, he noticed a significant decrease in his partner's stress level.

"I think it gave her a sense of relief that I was just as invested in our child's wellbeing as she was," Brad said.

Psychologist Dr. Kyle Pruett argues that a father's involvement in post-partum care builds mutual trust, makes the father more "connected" to the baby, and helps him to feel more confident in his role as a father.

Your little one is finally here, but with this joy comes many changes that can make the postpartum period challenging for both you and your partner. As a postpartum support specialist, I've compiled the most common questions, concerns, and struggles that dads may encounter and provided practical solutions, advice, and resources to help you confidently support your partner and bond with your new baby.

Common Questions and Concerns

1. **How can I support my partner through recovery?** Your partner has undergone a major physical and emotional event and will need time to heal. Offer to help with household chores, care for older children, and assist with breastfeeding if necessary.

2. **What can I do to bond with my new baby?** Babies are tiny and fragile, but there are many ways to bond with them. Try skin-to-skin contact, take turns feeding the baby with your partner, and practice baby-wearing. Playing soothing music or reading to the baby can also be great bonding experiences.

3. **How can I help my partner deal with postpartum depression or anxiety?** Listen to your partner, validate their feelings, and encourage them to seek professional help. Remember, postpartum depression can affect both parents.

Practical Solutions and Advice

1. **Practice open communication.** Share your feelings and concerns with your partner, and encourage them to do the same. Talking openly about your thoughts and feelings can strengthen your relationship and make you feel more connected.
2. **Be honest and vulnerable.** It's okay to admit when you're struggling or don't know what to do. Seeking help or admitting vulnerability is a sign of strength, not weakness.
3. **Be present and attentive.** Listen to your partner and offer physical and emotional support. Your partner will appreciate your presence and care.

The Importance of Communication and Vulnerability

Communication and vulnerability are essential for healthy relationships and family dynamics. Sharing your emotions and experiences during the postpartum period can encourage your partner to do the same and help you support each other better. Don't be afraid to ask for help or admit when struggling.

Pregnancy and the postpartum period can be a challenging time for individuals and families. It is important to prioritize mental health during this time, as perinatal mood and anxiety disorders can occur in up to 20% of women during pregnancy and after childbirth, according to the American Psychological Association. Seeking mental health support can improve mother, father, and child outcomes. Here are some of the top resources available for mental health support during the perinatal and postpartum period:

Postpartum Support International

Postpartum Support International (PSI) is dedicated to improving the emotional well-being of mothers, fathers, and their children. They offer a helpline, online support groups, and specialized resources such as their directory of mental health professionals. The helpline is available 24/7 and is staffed by trained and caring volunteers who offer support, confidential information, and local resources. They also have online support groups that can be accessed from anywhere worldwide.

Their directory of mental health professionals includes trained and knowledgeable therapists specializing in perinatal mental health. It is important to have a provider who understands the unique challenges of the perinatal period, and PSI's directory makes it easy to find such a provider.

National Fatherhood Initiative

The National Fatherhood Initiative offers courses and resources for fathers during the perinatal and postpartum periods. The courses cover various topics, including supporting the mother, managing work and home life, and bonding with the newborn. NFI also offers a blog, podcasts, and webinars that address topics of concern to men and fathers.

Being a new parent can also be challenging for fathers, and the National Fatherhood Initiative offers resources to support fathers during this time, allowing them to be the best fathers they can be.

National Suicide Prevention Lifeline

The National Suicide Prevention Lifeline is available 24/7 to provide support, resources, and hope for individuals experiencing suicidal thoughts or behaviors. They offer bilingual, deaf, hard-of-hearing support and a crisis chat service. It is important to note that emergency services should be contacted if immediate assistance is needed.

Suicidal ideation can be a common experience for individuals experiencing perinatal and postpartum mood and anxiety disorders. Having this resource available can be life-saving for individuals experiencing a crisis.

These resources are just a few examples of the support available to individuals and families during the perinatal and postpartum periods. Seeking mental health support can improve outcomes for all parties involved. It is important to remember that asking for and receiving help is okay.

Strategies to Balance Work and Family Life

The postpartum period can be busy, but balancing work and family commitments is important. Here are some strategies that can help:

1. **Create a schedule.** Establish a routine that works for you and your partner, and stick to it as much as possible.
2. **Be flexible.** Understand that your routine may change, and be willing to adapt as necessary.
3. **Take advantage of resources.** Consider using family-friendly work policies like flexible scheduling or parental leave to help you balance work and family commitments.

Coping Mechanisms for Sleep Deprivation and Limited Time for Self-care

Sleep deprivation and limited time for self-care are common struggles during the postpartum period. Here are some coping mechanisms that can help:

1. **Take naps.** Take turns napping with your partner or during the baby's nap times.
2. **Simplify your life.** Don't be afraid to say no to commitments and prioritize self-care activities like exercise or relaxing baths.
3. **Ask for help.** Contact family or friends for support, or consider hiring a postpartum doula or nanny to help with household chores or baby care.

The Effects of the Stigma Surrounding Men's Mental Health and Seeking Help for Postpartum Depression

Unfortunately, society often expects men to be strong and stoic, and seeking help for mental health issues can be stigmatized. However, it's important to remember that prioritizing and seeking help for your mental health is a sign of strength, not weakness. Talk openly about your struggles with your partner and healthcare provider, and seek professional help if necessary. Emotionally caring for yourself will make you a better partner and father.

The postpartum period can be a challenging time for dads. Still, with open communication, practical strategies, and ample resources, you can confidently support your partner and bond with your new baby. Remember to prioritize self-care and seek help when needed, and don't be afraid to admit vulnerability or ask for support.

Learn about postpartum care: Research what your partner is going through physically and emotionally during the postpartum period. This will help you support her better and give you a better idea of how you can be involved in your child's care.

Take on tasks: Help with diaper changes, bathing, burping, and feedings when you can. Taking on these tasks gives your partner some much-needed rest and bonding time with the baby.

Offer emotional support: Being there to listen, empathize, and support your partner can go a long way in mitigating the stress and anxiety that often accompany the postpartum period.

Connect with the baby: Take time to bond with your child through skin-to-skin contact, reading, or singing to them. This connection will have lifelong benefits for both you and your child.

By being involved in postpartum care, fathers can positively impact their own lives and the lives of their partners and children. It's time to break down the stigma around dads' involvement and acknowledge their invaluable role in postpartum care.

Common Questions And Concerns Dads Have About Postpartum Experiences

Bringing a child into the world is a significant milestone for any couple. However, the postpartum period can be challenging for new dads as they navigate their new roles and responsibilities. Here are some common questions dads may have about postpartum experiences:

What can I expect during the postpartum period?

The postpartum period can last several weeks after delivery, and it's essential to be prepared for the physical and emotional changes that new moms may experience. Your partner may have vaginal discharge, bleeding, sore breasts, and exhaustion from labor and delivery. Additionally, many new moms experience mood swings, anxiety, and postpartum depression.

How can I best support my partner during the postpartum period?

Dads can support their partner during the postpartum period in several ways, including helping with household chores, being empathetic and responsive to their partner's needs, encouraging bonding efforts between the baby and mom, and helping to calm the baby when possible. Taking charge of night feedings or diaper changes is also essential to help get mom much-needed rest.

How can I deal with sleep deprivation during the postpartum period?

Managing sleep deprivation can be a significant challenge for new parents. Two things that could help are taking turns with your partner regarding night feedings and diaper changes and encouraging your partner to nap during the day when the baby is sleeping.

How can I manage work and family responsibilities during the postpartum period?

Planning how to manage work and family responsibilities before and after the baby arrives is essential. This may include planning for a leave of absence if you must take time off work to be with your partner and new baby. If your partner is returning to work, make arrangements to care for the baby during that time. You may also consider hiring a babysitter or nanny to help with child care.

When should I seek professional help for postpartum depression?

If your partner is experiencing postpartum depression or other emotional changes affecting her ability to care for herself or the baby, seeking professional help is essential. If needed, encourage your partner to speak with her doctor or a mental health professional. Remember that it's natural to feel overwhelmed during the first few weeks of being new parents, and dads must support their partner emotionally and physically.

Emotional changes in women after birth

Besides the physical changes, many new moms experience emotional changes such as mood swings, anxiety, and postpartum depression. These emotional changes can be troubling for new moms, and dads must support their partners physically and emotionally.

How can dads support their partners during the postpartum period?

Dads need to be supportive of their partners during the postpartum period. Here are some ways dads can provide support:

- Help with household chores, including cooking and cleaning.
- Be empathetic and responsive to your partner's needs.

- Encourage and support bonding efforts between the baby and mom.
- Show affection through hugs, kisses, and holding hands.
- Help calm the baby when possible, for example, by rocking or soothing them to sleep.
- Take charge of night feedings or diaper changes to help get mom much-needed rest.

Dealing with sleep deprivation

One of the biggest challenges for new parents is managing sleep deprivation. Here are some tips for dads to help their partners get more rest:

- Take turns with your partner regarding night feedings and diaper changes.
- If possible, encourage your partner to nap during the day when the baby sleeps.
- Consider hiring a night nurse or nanny to help out.

Managing work and family responsibilities

Discussing and planning how to manage work and family responsibilities before and after the baby arrives is essential. Here are some things to consider:

- Plan a leave of absence if you must take time off work to be with your partner and new baby.
- If your partner is returning to work, make arrangements to care for the baby during that time.
- Consider hiring a babysitter or nanny to help with child care when your partner returns to work.

Seeking professional help if needed

If your partner is experiencing postpartum depression or other emotional changes affecting her ability to care for herself or the baby, seeking professional help is essential. If needed, encourage your partner to speak with her doctor or a mental health professional.

It's natural to feel overwhelmed during the first few weeks of being new parents, and dads must support their partners emotionally and physically. Remember that the postpartum period can last several weeks, and taking things one day at a time is essential. Congratulations again on your new bundle of joy!

Chapter 14

Understanding Postpartum

According to the American College of Obstetricians and Gynecologists, up to 80% of new mothers experience the baby blues. About 15% of new mothers will develop more severe postpartum depression, and men can experience similar symptoms. This statistic alone emphasizes the importance of understanding postpartum experiences and how we, as partners and caregivers, can support new moms during this time.

Understanding the postpartum period is crucial to supporting your partner and helping both of you navigate this new chapter in your lives. Through this chapter and the book, we hope to provide you with the knowledge and tools you need to understand this time better and support your partner fully.

What Happens To The Mother's Body After Childbirth

Becoming a father was one of the most incredible experiences of my life. I remember holding my son for the first time and feeling a new level of love and responsibility hit me all at once. As much as the focus is on the baby when a couple has a child, the mother also goes through a lot both during and after childbirth. It is essential to be aware of what happens to the mother's body after childbirth, so we can support the process and make the journey into motherhood as smooth as possible.

My wife, Penelope, had a relatively smooth delivery. However, the recovery process was a little harder than she had anticipated. Being first-time parents, we were both in the dark about what to expect after the baby's arrival. We learned a lot about the physical changes during and after pregnancy, including hormonal imbalances, postpartum bleeding, and breastfeeding challenges.

All fathers should know that a pregnant woman's body goes through many changes during pregnancy and doesn't just "snap back" after childbirth. Here are some of the most notable physical changes that occur:

Postpartum Bleeding

One of the most significant changes is postpartum bleeding when the uterus sheds the extra lining that grows to support the baby. It typically lasts a few weeks and can be significantly heavier than a regular period. She must wear pads, no tampons, take care of her perineum, and maintain good hygiene to prevent infections during this time.

Breastfeeding Challenges

Breastfeeding can also be challenging for new mothers. It can be painful and uncomfortable for the first few weeks. The advice and support of a lactation consultant can be invaluable during this time. Regular breastfeeding, good latching techniques, and using breast pads to avoid leaks can also help with this challenge.

Hormonal Imbalances

Hormonal changes during and after pregnancy can also cause significant physical and emotional changes. Hormonal imbalances can cause depression, anxiety, mood swings, and hair loss. New mothers need to prioritize self-care, involve their partner or family members in helping around the house, and talk to their doctor if they experience consistent negative feelings or other symptoms of anxiety or depression.

Urinary Incontinence

Another common issue is incontinence, which happens when the bladder hasn't fully recovered from childbirth. Women may leak urine when they laugh, sneeze, cough, or physically exert themselves. Kegel exercises can help strengthen the pelvic floor muscles and reduce incontinence. Use pads and make sure you practice good hygiene, and stay dry.

Back Pain

Back pain is also a common issue postpartum; carrying the baby or poor posture while breastfeeding can cause back pain. Being mindful of the baby's position during breastfeeding and stretching or engaging in low-impact physical activity can be helpful to prevent or alleviate such issues.

These changes can be overwhelming, and caring for the body and mind as they recover is essential. Here are some helpful tips for supporting women during this time of physical changes:

- Get sufficient rest while trying to avoid lying around all day. Ti's important to get up and move, especially as the body is recovering.
- Follow a nutritious diet that supports a healthy recovery.
- Encourage and support your partner in practicing self-care regularly.
- Take advantage of help from friends or family members to rest and recover.
- Communication is important. Share your feelings and struggles with someone you trust or a medical professional.

Postpartum recovery can be tough, but it's a natural process that a woman's body goes through after childbirth. Expectant parents should know the physical changes during pregnancy and what to expect after childbirth. With proper care, support, and patience, the mother and the baby can thrive during this exciting time.

How Hormones Affect The Mother's Mood And Behavior

As a new father, your primary focus is on your newborn, ensuring they are happy, healthy, and adjusting to life outside the womb. While this is important, it's essential to remember that your partner's body is also going through significant changes. One such change is the hormonal fluctuations during pregnancy and after childbirth, which can impact mood and behavior.

Understanding the hormonal changes in the mother's body during and after pregnancy is important to support your partner better.

Hormonal Changes

During pregnancy, the body experiences a significant increase in hormone production, including estrogen, progesterone, and oxytocin. Each of these hormones plays a unique role in supporting the mother and the developing baby.

- Estrogen: This hormone regulates mood and emotions, so its increase can lead to a more stable mood during pregnancy.
- Progesterone: Progesterone helps with the growth and development of the baby and can also lead to drowsiness and fatigue.
- Oxytocin: This hormone plays a role in stimulating contractions during labor and delivery and is also released during breastfeeding, helping to build the bond between mother and child.

After childbirth, hormone levels drop drastically, which can trigger postpartum mood disorders. Postpartum depression and anxiety are the most common mood disorders that affect new mothers, causing symptoms such as irritability, mood swings, excessive worry, and difficulty sleeping.

Supporting Your Partner

It's essential to remember that every woman experiences hormonal changes differently. However, there are some things you can do as a partner to help alleviate the intensity of mood swings and anxiety.

1. Normalizing feelings: Explain to your partner that mood swings and anxiety are common after childbirth and that she is not alone. Encourage her to talk to friends or join support groups to connect with other mothers who have gone through similar experiences.
2. Encouraging self-care practices: Pregnancy and childbirth can take a toll on a woman's physical and mental health, so encourage your partner to prioritize self-care practices such as taking a relaxing bath, going for a walk, or practicing meditation or yoga.
3. Supporting healthy eating and exercise habits: A balanced diet and regular exercise can help alleviate symptoms of postpartum mood disorders. Encourage your partner to eat nutritious meals and engage in low-impact physical activity.
4. Providing practical support: Errands, caretaking, housework, and cooking can overwhelm new mothers. Offer to help with chores around the house or give her a break by taking the baby for a few hours so she can have time to rest.
5. Seeking professional help: If symptoms of postpartum depression or anxiety persist, encourage your partner to seek professional help. This can include therapy, group counseling, or medication, and do your best to support her in this decision.

Remember, it's natural for new mothers to experience hormonal changes after childbirth, and you can support your partner during this time in many ways. The key is understanding, patience, and willingness to provide the support she needs as she adjusts to life with a newborn.

Symptoms And Signs Of Postpartum Depression And Anxiety

Becoming a new dad is an exciting and life-changing experience. However, it's not all sunshine and rainbows. Many new dads experience postpartum depression and anxiety but often go undiagnosed and untreated.

Postpartum depression and anxiety are mood disorders that can affect new mothers and fathers. Caused by physical and emotional factors, it can be challenging to identify the symptoms and signs. However, it's essential to educate yourself on postpartum depression and anxiety to identify when and if you're experiencing it.

What is Postpartum Depression and Anxiety?

Postpartum depression is a mood disorder that can occur after the birth of a child. It's estimated that 1 in 10 new fathers will experience postpartum depression and anxiety.

Symptoms include:

- Mood swings and irritability.
- Extreme feelings of sadness and hopelessness.
- Lack of interest in activities you once enjoyed.
- Loss of appetite or overeating.
- Sleep disturbances.
- Fatigue or loss of energy.
- Feelings of worthlessness or guilt.
- Social isolation.
- Difficulty bonding with the baby.

Postpartum anxiety is also a common mood disorder among new parents. Symptoms include:

- Feeling nervous or anxious.
- Excessive worrying about the baby's health and well-being.
- Irritability or agitation.
- Racing thoughts.
- Panic attacks.
- Difficulty sleeping.

It's possible to mistake the signs and symptoms of postpartum depression and anxiety for "baby blues." However, if you notice any of the symptoms above lasting for more than two weeks, it's time to take them seriously and seek help.

It's essential to seek professional advice from your doctor or mental health professional to help you determine if you are experiencing postpartum depression or anxiety.

Coping Strategies

If you think you might be experiencing postpartum depression or anxiety, there are some practical things you can do to manage your symptoms:

1. Prioritize sleep: It's essential to get enough sleep to help manage mood swings, feelings of irritability, and fatigue. This can be difficult for new fathers, but it's important to try and find time to rest whenever possible.
2. Regular exercise: Exercise has been shown to reduce symptoms of depression and anxiety. You don't need to engage in high-intensity exercise; something as simple as walking with your baby can help.
3. Connect with your partner: Connect with your partner and share your thoughts and feelings openly. It's important to create an environment that allows you both to talk about the challenges of raising a child and seek support and validation.
4. Seek professional help: Don't be afraid to ask for professional help. Your doctor or mental health professional can recommend therapy, medication, or support groups to help you manage your symptoms.

5. Practice self-care: Prioritize self-care practices such as meditation, deep breathing, journaling, or other hobbies that help you take care of yourself and manage stress.

It's essential to understand that postpartum depression and anxiety are common mental health disorders that can affect new fathers. Educate yourself on the signs and symptoms, and seek professional help when necessary. Practicing healthy habits such as sleep, exercise, and self-care can help manage symptoms and reduce the impact on your mental and physical health. Remember, you are not alone; resources are available to help you through this challenging time.

Stigma Surrounding Mental Health And Seeking Help

As a new father, it's easy to get caught up in the chaos of parenthood. You're sleep-deprived, stressed out, and trying your best to keep everything together. But what happens when it all becomes too much to handle? What if you start experiencing symptoms of depression, anxiety, or burnout?

Unfortunately, mental health issues are often stigmatized in our society, and new fathers are not immune to this. Many people still see mental illness as a weakness, making it difficult for new fathers to seek the help they need. But here's the truth: mental health struggles are common, and seeking help is a sign of strength, not weakness.

If you're a new father struggling with your mental health, there are some warning signs you should be aware of. These can include sadness or hopelessness, a lack of interest in things you used to enjoy, changes in appetite or sleep patterns, and difficulty concentrating. If you're experiencing any of these symptoms, seeking help is important.

So what can you do to get the support you need? Start by talking to your partner, a trusted friend, or a doctor. Many resources are also available to new fathers, including therapy, support groups, and online communities. Don't be afraid to seek help – you're not alone.

As society becomes more open and accepting of mental health issues, we can start to break down the stigma surrounding these struggles. We can create a world where new fathers feel empowered to seek the help they need when they need it – without fear of judgment or shame.

If you're a new father struggling with mental health issues, know it's okay not to be okay. Reach out for help; remember, there is hope for a brighter tomorrow. Together, we can work towards a future where mental health struggles are met with compassion and understanding.

How Postpartum Depression Affects The Whole Family

You never thought it could happen to you. You were so excited to become a father, hold your little ones in your arms, and watch them grow and learn. But now that the baby is here, everything feels different. Your partner is struggling with postpartum depression, and you're unsure how to help.

Postpartum depression is a complex and misunderstood condition affecting many new mothers. Various factors, including changes in hormone levels, sleep deprivation, and a lack of support, can trigger it. But many people don't realize that postpartum depression can also affect fathers, albeit differently.

As a father, you're dealing with many emotions right now. You're happy and proud of your new family but also overwhelmed and anxious about the responsibilities that come with it. Watching your partner struggle with postpartum depression can be heartbreaking, and feeling helpless and frustrated is natural.

But here's the thing – you're not helpless. There are things you can do to support your partner and help your family get through this difficult time. Here are a few strategies to keep in mind:

1. Educate yourself: Learn more about postpartum depression and its symptoms. Talk to your partner's doctor or a mental health professional who can provide insight and guidance.
2. Communicate openly: Encourage your partner to be open and listen to their feelings without judgment. Let them know that you're there to support and love them.

3. Prioritize self-care: Taking care of yourself is important too. Ensure you're getting enough sleep, eating well, and taking time to relax and recharge.

4. Seek help: If your partner's symptoms are severe or persist for over a few weeks, seek professional help. Many resources are available, including therapy, support groups, and medications.

Remember, postpartum depression is neither your fault nor your partner's fault. It's a medical condition that requires treatment and support. By working together and seeking help when needed, you can help your partner and family get through this difficult time.

Postpartum depression is tough, but you're tougher. With the right resources and support, you and your partner can overcome this obstacle and emerge stronger on the other side.

How Fathers Can Support Their Partners Through Postpartum Depression

Becoming a father can be an exciting and fulfilling experience but also overwhelming and stressful. One of the challenges you may face as a first-time father is supporting your partner through postpartum depression. This condition affects up to 1 in 7 women and can significantly impact your partner's emotional and physical well-being. Here are some tips and strategies to help support your partner through this difficult time.

Recognizing Postpartum Depression

Postpartum depression can manifest in different ways, but common symptoms include:

- Extreme sadness, hopelessness, or feelings of worthlessness
- Difficulty sleeping or excessive sleeping
- Changes in appetite

- Fatigue and low energy
- Loss of interest in once enjoyable activities
- Difficulty bonding with the baby

If your partner is experiencing any of these symptoms, taking action is essential. Remember that postpartum depression is a disease, and it requires medical attention. Encourage your partner to talk to her doctor, a mental health professional, or a support group for new mothers.

Communicating with Your Partner

Communication is key to supporting your partner through postpartum depression. Be present with your partner and listen to her carefully without judgment or interruption. Encourage her to express her feelings and emotions, and reassure her that you're there for her.

It's also essential to be aware of your own emotions and feelings. As a new father, you may be experiencing a range of emotions, including anxiety, fatigue, and stress. It's okay to feel overwhelmed but try not to let these emotions interfere with your ability to support your partner. If you need help, don't hesitate to contact a mental health professional or a support group for new fathers.

Supporting Your Partner

There are many ways you can support your partner through postpartum depression. Here are some strategies that may help:

- Help around the house: Caring for a new baby is full-time, and your partner may feel overwhelmed and exhausted. Offer to do household chores, such as cleaning or cooking, to ease the burden.
- Take care of the baby: Spend time with your baby and take on some of the responsibilities related to their care. This will give your partner some time to rest and recharge.

- Encourage self-care: Encourage your partner to care for herself physically and mentally. This can include getting enough sleep, exercising, and eating well.
- Seek professional help: If your partner's symptoms are severe or persist for over a few weeks, seek professional help. Many treatment options include therapy, support groups, and medication.

Advice from Other Fathers and Experts

Here are some quotes from other fathers and experts in the field of postpartum depression:

- "As a father, being there for your partner, listening, and providing support is essential. It's okay to feel overwhelmed, but remember that your partner needs you now more than ever." - John, father of two
- "Postpartum depression is a disease, and it's not something that women can just 'snap out of.' It's essential to seek professional help and provide a supportive and understanding environment for your partner." - Jane, mother of three
- "It's okay not to have all the answers or know exactly what to do. Being there for your partner and seeking professional help is the most important thing that you can do." - Tom, father of one

Supporting your partner through postpartum depression can be challenging, but it's a vital role that you need to play as a father. Remember to communicate openly and support your partner without judgment or criticism, and don't forget to take care of yourself. With time, patience, and professional help, you and your partner can overcome postpartum depression and emerge stronger as a family.

Chapter 15

Navigating The First Few Weeks

The first few weeks of fatherhood can be both exciting and overwhelming. You've probably already experienced various emotions, from pure joy to exhaustion. Don't worry; it's all normal.

Emotional and Physical Changes

As a new father, you may experience various emotions, including joy, excitement, fear, and anxiety. It's okay to feel overwhelmed or unsure of what to do. You're not alone. More so, you are just like everyone who became a father for the first time, and everyone is always doing their best.

You may also experience physical changes, such as fatigue, sleep deprivation, and changes in your appetite. Make sure you're taking care of yourself during this time. Try to get as much rest as possible, especially when the baby sleeps. And remember to feed and hydrate yourself consistently and eat a balanced diet to help boost your energy levels.

Bonding With Your Baby

Bonding with your baby is essential and might not come immediately. It takes time and effort to develop a bond with your baby. Don't be disheartened if you don't feel an instant connection. It's normal, and you will form a bond with your baby over time.

Here are some things you can do to strengthen your bond with your newborn:

- Skin-to-skin contact: Holding your baby skin-to-skin can help promote bonding.
- Talking and singing: Talk to your baby and sing to them; they will recognize your voice and find it comforting.
- Helping with diaper changes: Help with diaper changes and other aspects of the baby's care. This will allow you to bond with your baby while helping out your partner.

Supporting The Mother

Supporting your partner during the first few weeks of fatherhood is essential. They've been through a lot physically and emotionally and might need much support. Here are some tips on how to do it:

- Take on some of the household responsibilities: Your partner will appreciate it if you help with household chores, such as cooking, cleaning, or laundry.
- Be available: Be willing to help with the baby. You can take care of the baby, feed them, or offer some much-needed breaks to your partner.
- Give her some time to herself: Your partner will appreciate some time to herself. Encourage her to nap, read a book, or spend time with friends.

Remember, communicating with your partner and having a strong support network is key to surviving the first few weeks of fatherhood. Don't hesitate to reach out to your friends, neighbors, or family who already have experience in parenting to learn more about parenthood.

As a first-time father, I encourage you to take advantage of every moment spent with your newborn. They grow so fast, and every moment spent with them is precious. Take pictures, record videos, and write down your thoughts and emotions. You will appreciate looking back at these keepsakes in years to come.

Lastly, I encourage you to enjoy the moment. It's a challenging but also joyful phase of life.

Being there for your partner during the postpartum period is crucial: it's a time of physical and emotional changes for both of you as you adapt to your new roles as parents. As a first-time father, I found the experience both challenging and exciting. I remember feeling exhausted and uncertain about my abilities, but with my partner, we found ways to support each other and navigate the challenges.

Here are some tips I learned along the way:

Expect the unexpected: The postpartum period is a rollercoaster of emotions for your partner. They may feel on an emotional rollercoaster from sleep deprivation to hormonal shifts. Knowing what to expect can help you prepare and respond with empathy and care.

Listen and support: Listening actively and without judgment is important if your partner needs to vent, cry or express joy. To show you care, offer practical support, such as taking on household tasks, cooking, or running errands.

Be involved in childcare: Taking care of the baby together can help you bond as a family and give your partner a break. Try feeding, changing diapers, or engaging in playtime with the baby.

Stay connected: It's easy to prioritize the baby's needs and forget about your relationship with your partner. Make an effort to spend quality time together, even just a few minutes daily. Plan a cozy, romantic date night, or do something you enjoy.

Seek help when needed: Parenting can be overwhelming, and knowing when to ask for help is important. Don't hesitate to reach out if you need advice from a pediatrician or support from family or friends.

Remember, caring for your partner postpartum is a team effort. With patience, love, and support, you can ease into your new roles as parents and enjoy this exciting chapter in your lives.

Coping With Sleep Deprivation And Lack Of Time For Self-Care

Becoming a father can be one of the most rewarding experiences, but it can also be challenging. Sleep deprivation and lack of time for self-care can impact your overall health and well-being. It's essential to prioritize taking care of yourself to be healthy and happy for your family.

As a first-time father, I fully understand the meaning of sleep deprivation. I remember feeling exhausted, drained, and irritable most of the time. I also found it challenging to find time for myself, impacting my mental health and relationships with my family.

I realized that, as a father, there is a lot of pressure, and self-care is essential. When I began to prioritize self-care, everything fell into place. I began approaching fatherhood with new vigor because self-care made me feel physically and mentally better.

Coping Strategies

Mindfulness Techniques

Mindfulness techniques can help calm your mind and reduce anxiety. You can try simple breathing exercises or meditation practice when you have short periods, in line at the store, or even during late-night feedings.

Prioritize

Prioritizing tasks can help you manage your time and help you make the most out of each day. Each day, create a to-do list and categorize the tasks according to their urgency. You'll feel a sense of accomplishment when you cross each item off the list.

Ask for Help

Don't be afraid to ask for help when you need it. Consider asking friends, relatives, or neighbors for help with childcare or errands. Hiring a babysitter can also help you have some much-needed time for yourself.

Why It's Important

Prioritizing self-care is essential to your overall health and well-being, but it's also necessary for your family's health and happiness. When you care for yourself, you can be present and attentive to your family. This, in turn, makes your family happy and satisfied.

Being a father is challenging, but prioritizing self-care makes it much easier. I advise you to take time for yourself, no matter how small it seems. Spend some quiet time alone, walk, work out, or have coffee with friends. A little self-care for you can go a long way for your family.

Changes In Priorities And Dealing With New Responsibilities

You'll experience various emotions, and your priorities will shift after welcoming your newborn.

Emotions

Feeling overwhelmed, unsure, and nervous is normal during the first few months of fatherhood. However, remember that all emotions are valid and a part of adapting to fatherhood. Try talking to a friend or therapist if you feel anxious or sad. Sharing your emotions can often be cathartic and help you gain perspective.

Relationships

Becoming a father also shifts relationship dynamics. You'll need to balance your relationship with your partner and your new responsibilities as a father. Communicating and working together are essential to handle your new roles. Spending quality time together and enjoying shared interests can help maintain vital intimacy and connection in relationships.

Priorities

With the addition of a newborn, your priorities will undoubtedly shift. It's important to prioritize family time and balance work, self-care, and leisure. Finding a balance can be challenging as a first-time father, but as you gain experience and become more comfortable in your role, you'll find it easier to balance all aspects of your life.

Challenges

As a first-time father, you might encounter challenges such as sleep deprivation, the anxiety of being a good parent, and adjustments to your daily routine. It's essential to remember that you're not alone in this.

Here are some tips on navigating these challenges:

- Sleep deprivation can be challenging, but you can try to manage it by coordinating with your partner to split baby duties and considering taking sleep breaks during the day.
- Remember there's no perfect way to be a father, and asking for help is okay. Contact family, friends, or professionals when you need guidance or assistance.
- Adjusting to a new routine can be challenging, but staying flexible and adaptable is crucial. Expect to change your schedule to fit your new role and responsibilities.

As a first-time father, I understand the challenges and joys associated with fatherhood. One critical piece of advice I would share is to enjoy the journey. It's a remarkable experience to witness your child's growth and development. Additionally, try to find moments of joy and laughter with your new family - they will serve as heartwarming memories. Always be present and take your time to cherish every special moment.

Navigating your journey as a first-time father is an emotional and transformative experience. Ensure you take care of yourself and communicate effectively with your partner. Keeping a flexible schedule and asking for assistance when needed can help you stay in control during this phase of life. Remember to savor each moment, as it's a journey you will never forget.

Bonding With The New Baby

Becoming a father for the first time can be an overwhelming experience, but it's also an opportunity to bond with your newborn meaningfully. Here are tips for establishing a strong connection with your baby.

Physical Touch and Holding

Physical touch and holding your baby are great ways to bond with them. Skin-to-skin contact helps produce the hormone oxytocin, which aids bonding and has several health benefits. Try to hold your baby as much as possible, cuddle them, or stroke their cheek or hand.

Soothing a Crying Baby

Crying is a natural way for your baby to communicate with you. If your baby is crying and you can't figure out why, try these soothing techniques:

- Gently rock or sway your baby
- Hold your baby close and pat them gently
- Walk around with your baby

- Sing a soothing song to your baby

Talking and Singing to the Baby

Talking and singing to your baby can be a great bonding experience. Babies respond to sounds and find them calming. Start by talking to your baby while changing their diaper or bathing them. Explain what you're doing or share a story. Sing lullabies, nursery rhymes, or songs that you love. Your baby will enjoy the sound of your voice, and it's a great way to bond.

Diaper Changing

Diaper changing is a great opportunity for fathers to bond with their newborns. Keep this time playful and fun. Talk to your baby, make funny faces or sounds, and sing a song. Additionally, take your time and be gentle when cleaning them. Also, when possible, try to have an unobstructed view of your baby's face so you can maintain eye contact while changing their diaper.

Feeding

Feeding your baby is an essential bonding experience. Whether you're breastfeeding or bottle-feeding, try to hold your baby close, make eye contact or sings a lullaby gently. This is also an ideal opportunity to practice skin-to-skin contact.

As a first-time father, I understand the importance of bonding with your newborn. I remember feeling nervous when holding my baby and changing their diaper for the first time, but as I practiced more, it became more natural, and I enjoyed the bonding experience much more.

Also, I found that as my baby grew, reading stories or playing peek-a-boo became our favorite activity. Don't be scared to be silly and make fun of your baby; babies love playful moments.

Bonding with your newborn is an essential component of parenthood.

Therefore, being present and engaging actively with your baby is important. Focus on physical touch, such as holding your baby, singing and reading to them, soothing them in times of distress, and spending time with them during diaper changes and feedings. Remember, over time, you'll find your rhythm and a bonding experience that works best for you and your baby.

Incorporating Self-Care Routines Into The New Routine

As a new father, you may feel like there's no time for anything other than caring for your little bundle of joy. It's easy to fall into a routine of putting your needs aside in favor of your child's. However, it's important to prioritize your self-care and make time for it in your daily routine. Not only will it benefit your mental and physical health, but it will also make you a better father.

Self-care is essential for maintaining your well-being as a new father. It can encompass a variety of practices, including exercise, eating healthy, practicing mindfulness, and getting enough sleep. Taking care of yourself will not only help you to stay physically healthy, but it will also help to reduce stress, increase happiness, and improve your overall quality of life.

As a new father, it can be challenging to incorporate self-care into your daily routine. Between diaper changes, feedings, and limited sleep, it may seem like there's no time left for anything else. However, by consciously prioritizing your self-care, you can reap the benefits of a healthier, more balanced lifestyle.

Step-by-Step Guide to Incorporating Self-Care

To help you get started on your self-care journey, here are some step-by-step guidelines to follow:

Start Small

Don't overwhelm yourself by trying to implement too many changes at once. Start small by incorporating one self-care practice at a time. For example, you could start by taking a 10-minute walk each day or practicing deep breathing exercises for a few minutes before bed.

Schedule Your Self-Care Time

Like you schedule time for your baby's feedings and naps, schedule time for self-care, whether it's a daily yoga session or a weekly outing with friends, block off time on your calendar to ensure you follow through.

Involve Your Partner

Self-care doesn't have to be a solo activity. Involve your partner in your self-care routine by watching the baby while the other takes time to relax or exercise.

Make it a Habit

Consistency is key when it comes to incorporating self-care into your routine. Make it a habit by committing to your self-care routine for at least 21 days.

Exercise

- Take a daily walk with your baby in the stroller
- Join a dad's fitness group or gym
- Incorporate home workouts into your routine

Mindfulness and Relaxation

- Practice deep breathing exercises
- Meditate for a few minutes each day
- Take a relaxing bath or shower

Social Connection

- Connect with other first-time fathers through local parenting groups
- Schedule time to spend with friends or family
- Join an online support group for dads

Hobbies

- Pursue a hobby that you enjoy, such as reading, painting, or playing an instrument
- Start a DIY project around the house
- Try a new hobby, such as cooking or gardening

It's important to prioritize self-care to maintain mental and physical health. While it may seem challenging to incorporate self-care into your daily routine, following these step-by-step guidelines and trying out some of the self-care ideas listed above can make it a habit and start reaping the benefits. Remember, taking care of yourself will not only benefit you, but it will also make you a better father.

Chapter 16

The Challenges Of Parenthood

Becoming a new dad brings a lot of joy, but it can also bring many challenges. In this chapter, we will explore some common challenges that new dads face and provide insights and advice on overcoming them. From adjusting to your new role as a parent to navigating the postpartum period, we'll cover various topics to help you feel confident and empowered as a new dad. Remember, navigating the challenges of parenthood is a journey, but with the right tools and mindset, you can tackle anything that comes your way.

Balancing Work And Family Life During The Postpartum Period

As you embark on this journey, you'll quickly realize that parenting is a roller coaster ride with ups and downs that no one can prepare you for. However, fear not! This chapter will explore your challenges and provide tips for overcoming them.

As a first-time father, you'll face many challenges, including sleep deprivation, changing relationships with your partner, and the overwhelming responsibility of caring for a newborn. It can be tough at times, but trust me, the rewards of fatherhood are immeasurable.

Throughout this chapter, I'll share my personal experiences with you empathetically to help you navigate the rough waters of fatherhood. We'll delve into the importance of self-care, ways to establish a support system, and, most importantly, how to remain engaged with your partner. The skills you'll learn here will help you adjust to your new role and strengthen your family unit.

Remember, embracing the challenges of parenthood is vital to becoming the best dad you can be. So, settle in and get ready to tackle the challenges head-on. You've got this!

Understanding Different Communication Styles

Before you can effectively communicate with your child, it's important to recognize that everyone has a different communication style. Some people are direct, while others communicate indirectly. Some people are emotional, while others are more analytical. By understanding your communication style and your child's, you can adjust your approach to improve your communication.

Expressing Emotions Effectively

As a father, it's important to express your emotions healthily. Feeling overwhelmed or frustrated is okay, but it's important not to take it out on your child. Instead, take a break and gather your thoughts before returning to the conversation with a clear mind. Additionally, try using "I" statements rather than "you" when expressing your emotions. For example, saying "I feel overwhelmed" instead of "You are overwhelming me" is less accusatory and more effective.

Active Listening Techniques

Effective communication isn't just about expressing yourself; it's also about actively listening to others. When your child is communicating with you, make sure you give them your full attention. Avoid multitasking or interrupting them. Instead, listen actively, ask questions to clarify, and validate their feelings.

Developing Empathy

Empathy is a powerful communication tool that helps build strong connections. Putting yourself in your child's shoes and trying to understand their perspective can develop a deeper connection and strengthen your bond. To do this, imagine how your child feels and validate their emotions. Saying things like "I can understand why you feel that way" or "I would be upset too if that happened to me" can go a long way in developing empathy.

How These Skills Can Help in the Father-Child Relationship

Effective communication skills are essential in building a strong bond between you and your child. Using these skills, you can communicate respectfully and empathetically. This, in turn, helps your child feel heard and understood, leading to a stronger and more positive relationship.

Developing effective communication skills is essential for any father who wants to build a strong bond with their child. By understanding different communication styles, expressing your emotions effectively, actively listening, and developing empathy, you can build a strong foundation of communication that will benefit both you and your child in the present and for years to come.

Coping With Feelings Of Isolation And Being Left Out

Coping with feelings of isolation and being left out can be particularly difficult, especially as you navigate this new chapter. But rest assured. You're not alone.

Many first-time fathers experience this emotion, and it's essential to understand how to cope with these feelings effectively. Here are some insights and actionable advice to help support you through this journey.

Understanding Why You Feel Isolated and Left Out

First, it's essential to recognize that feeling isolated and left out is entirely normal. Fatherhood is a unique experience that comes with many changes, and it's normal to feel overwhelmed or disconnected from your usual routine and relationships.

It's also common to feel that you're not connecting with your child as well as your partner is or that you're not a significant part of the new family dynamic. Remember that building a bond with your child takes time, and it's okay to feel like you're still figuring things out.

Building a Support System

Building a support system is one of the best ways to cope with feelings of isolation and being left out. You can start by discussing your feelings with your partner, close friends, and family. Having someone to confide in and support you through this journey is essential.

You can also find resources that cater specifically to first-time fathers. Check online communities, parenting groups, and classes in your area. Connecting with other first-time fathers experiencing similar emotions can be comforting and empowering.

Seeking Professional Help

If you struggle to cope with these emotions, don't hesitate to seek professional help. There's no shame in contacting a therapist, counselor, or support group for fathers. Talking to a professional can provide valuable insights and tools to help you cope and manage your emotions effectively.

Being a first-time father is an amazing experience, but it's also valid to feel isolated and left out. Remember that reaching out for support and seeking professional help when necessary is a sign of strength. Building a support system and finding resources catered to first-time fathers can also be beneficial. Always remember, you're not alone in this journey.

Dealing With Societal Expectations And Pressures

Becoming a first-time father is an incredible moment filled with many emotions - happiness, excitement, and pride. As you hold your newborn child, you realize the weight of the responsibility that comes with fatherhood. You also become acutely aware of the societal expectations and pressures placed on you as a new father.

Gender Roles and Responsibilities

Societal expectations for fathers have changed, but outdated gender roles and responsibilities still linger. There's an idea that fathers must be the family's breadwinners, providers, and protectors. This outdated view can be incredibly stressful, especially if you don't meet these expectations.

Pressures That Come with This New Role

Many pressures come with being a father, both financially and emotionally. Financial stress can come from the added expenses of having a child, while emotional stress can come from trying to balance work and family life. On top of that, fathers face societal judgments, such as expectations to be more involved in their children's lives or the pressure to perform traditionally maternal roles.

How to Cope with Societal Expectations and Pressures

As a new father, you must recognize that you are not alone in navigating societal expectations and pressures. The first step is acknowledging how these expectations and pressures make you feel. Being honest with yourself and your partner about coping with these stresses is essential.

It's also crucial to prioritize self-care. This means setting aside time to recharge, whether spending time with friends or pursuing a hobby you enjoy. Don't be afraid to seek support from your partner or a professional if you struggle to cope. Remember, asking for help is a sign of strength.

Finally, it's important to stay true to yourself and your family. Don't feel you must conform to outdated gender roles or societal expectations. Be involved in your child's life in a way that feels authentic to you, and prioritize your family's needs over outside pressures.

Navigating societal expectations and pressures as a first-time father can be challenging, but it's important to remember that you're not alone. Take the time to acknowledge your feelings and prioritize self-care. Seek support from your partner or a professional if needed. Most importantly, stay true to yourself and your family. With patience, self-care, and a commitment to your family's needs, you can navigate the societal expectations and pressures of fatherhood.

Addressing The Lack Of Support And Acknowledgment For Dads During The Postpartum Period

As you embark on this exciting journey, it's important to recognize the challenges of the postpartum period. While there's a lot of focus on supporting new mothers during this time, fathers often feel left out and unsupported.

Your Experience as a First-Time Father

As a first-time father, you may feel like your role in the postpartum period is limited to providing practical support for your partner and caring for your new baby. While these roles are essential, it's important to recognize the emotional impact that this period can have on fathers.

You may feel overwhelmed, stressed, and anxious about your new role as a parent. The lack of support and acknowledgment for dads during the postpartum period can exacerbate these feelings and make coping difficult.

Advocating for Dads During the Postpartum Period

It's time to change the narrative and advocate for fathers during the postpartum period. Fathers play an essential role in the early days of a child's life and deserve support and acknowledgment for their contributions.

It's essential to start speaking up about the lack of support and acknowledgment for dads during this period. This can involve talking to your partner, family, and friends about your experiences, advocating for family-friendly policies in your workplace, and getting involved in support groups for new fathers.

The Importance of Support and Acknowledgment for Dads

Support and acknowledgment during the postpartum period can significantly impact your mental and emotional well-being. This adjustment can help you feel valued, appreciated, and connected with your family.

By seeking out support and advocating for yourself and other fathers, you're improving your experience and helping to create a more inclusive and supportive environment for fathers in the future.

The lack of support and acknowledgment for dads during the postpartum period is a real issue, but we can make a difference by speaking up and advocating for change. As a first-time father, it's important to recognize your experiences and seek the support you need. Remember, you play an essential role in your child's life, and you deserve support and acknowledgment for your contributions during this exciting and challenging time.

Chapter 17

Navigating Through the Storm

Hey there, first-time dad. Are you feeling overwhelmed, anxious, or exhausted after the arrival of your little one? You are not alone. Postpartum depression and anxiety affect not only new moms but dads as well. Feeling this way is okay; you don't have to suffer silently.

We understand that taking the first step towards seeking help can be daunting, but remember that it's an act of bravery. Your mental health matters, and it's essential to prioritize it just as much as your new parenting responsibilities. We'll guide you through practical self-care strategies to help you cope with this challenging time.

This chapter will empower you with knowledge and encouragement to face and overcome postpartum depression and anxiety. You are a fantastic dad who will overcome this storm with the right support.

Strategies For Managing Stress And Anxiety

Congratulations on becoming a father! It's a beautiful and life-changing experience but can be stressful and anxiety-inducing. As a new dad, I understand the pressures and challenges that come with parenting, and I want to offer you some practical tips to help manage the stress and anxiety accompanying it.

Relaxation Techniques

One of the best ways to manage stress and anxiety is by practicing relaxation techniques. Deep breathing, progressive muscle relaxation, and guided imagery are all excellent methods for calming the mind and reducing tension in the body.

Example: Before bed, try lying down and taking a few deep breaths, inhaling through your nose, and exhaling through your mouth. Pay attention to how your body feels as you breathe and release any tension with each exhale.

Mindfulness Exercises

Mindfulness is the practice of being present at the moment and observing your thoughts and feelings without judgment. It's an effective way to reduce stress and anxiety and increase feelings of calm and clarity.

Example: While feeding or playing with your child, focus solely on your interaction with them. Notice the sensations you feel as you hold them, the sounds they make, and their small movements with their hands and feet.

Communication Strategies

Communication is essential in managing stress and anxiety. Talking with your partner, friends, or family members about your feelings can help you process your emotions and feel supported.

Example: Schedule a weekly check-in with your partner where you both have time to share your feelings and struggles. Make it a priority to listen to each other actively and offer support and encouragement.

Take Breaks

Parenting can be exhausting, and taking time for yourself is essential. Whether it's a few minutes of quiet meditation, a solo walk around the block, or indulging in your favorite hobby, taking breaks can help recharge your batteries and reduce stress.

Example: Set aside 15 minutes daily to meditate or take a short walk alone, away from distractions or responsibilities.

Managing stress and anxiety takes practice and commitment, but finding balance and peace in your new role as a father is possible with the right techniques and support. Remember to be kind to yourself and seek help when you need it. You've got this!

Reaching Out for Help

Being a new father is an incredible experience and incredibly challenging. Postpartum depression is a real and common experience, and feeling over-whelmed and struggling is okay. It's important to remember that postpartum depression is not your fault, and help is available.

Recognizing the Signs and Symptoms

Postpartum depression can manifest itself in many different ways. You may feel sad, anxious, irritable, or not like yourself. Some fathers experience physical symptoms, such as headaches or a lack of energy. You may have difficulty sleeping or eating regularly. These symptoms can begin shortly after your child is born or may not develop for several months or even a year.

It's important to understand that these feelings are valid and nothing to be ashamed of, but that doesn't mean you must suffer in silence. Speaking to someone about what you're going through can help tremendously.

Reaching Out for Help

Many resources are available to new fathers suffering from postpartum depression. One option is to seek therapy either individually or with your partner. This can be an excellent way to learn coping strategies and discuss your emotions and challenges.

Another option is medication. Depression is a medical condition, and sometimes medication is necessary to manage it. A doctor can work with you to find the right medication and dosage.

Support groups are another valuable resource. You can connect with other fathers going through similar challenges and share experiences and advice. These groups can be in person or online.

Finding the Right Help for You

Speaking to a mental health professional who can help you determine the best course of action for your particular situation is important. They can refer you to a therapist or support group or help you find the right medication.

An Uplifting Message

Remember, you are not alone. Many new fathers experience postpartum depression, and it's not a sign of weakness to seek help. It takes incredible courage to admit that you need assistance, and doing so is the first step toward recovery.

If you or your partner are experiencing postpartum depression, know that there is hope and recovery is possible. You can overcome this challenge and be your best father with the right treatment and support.

Remember to take care of yourself, prioritize your mental health, and don't be shy about seeking the help you need. You got this!

Coping with Distressing Emotions and Thoughts

When I became a father, I was over the moon with happiness. My wife and I were ecstatic when we discovered we were expecting. However, I also had some worries and fears I didn't expect to feel. I was concerned if I would be a good father if I would be able to provide for my family, and if I would be able to handle the responsibilities of fatherhood. Having these thoughts and emotions is normal and part of the process.

Self-Doubt

Self-doubt is one of the most common emotions that first-time fathers experience. You have never been a dad before and may feel unprepared for it. You may feel like you are not doing a good enough job or not providing enough for your child. This doubt can eat away at you if you let it.

The truth is that you are doing the best that you can. Becoming a father is a learning process, and adjusting to your new role takes time. Don't be too hard on yourself; don't be afraid to ask for help. You are not alone in this journey; plenty of resources are available to assist you.

Anxiety

Anxiety is another common emotion that first-time fathers experience. You may worry about your child's safety, your partner's health, and your family's financial situation. These worries can consume your thoughts and make it difficult to enjoy the time you have with your new addition.

One way to cope with this anxiety is to take care of yourself. Prioritize healthy habits like exercise, meditation, and proper sleep hygiene. By taking care of yourself, you can better manage the stresses of fatherhood.

Sleep Deprivation

Sleep deprivation is a widespread issue among new parents. Getting enough rest is hard when your little one cries throughout the night. Lack of sleep can affect your mood, energy levels, and overall health. It's essential to try to get as much rest as possible, even if it's not in long stretches.

One way to cope with sleep deprivation is to take turns with your partner. Try alternating the nights that you get up to comfort your little one. This way, you both get at least one good night's sleep every few days.

Changes in Relationships

Becoming a father can also bring changes to your relationships. Communicating with your partner, family, and friends about these changes is important. They may not understand the demands of being a father and setting boundaries to manage expectations is important.

Making time for yourself and your partner as a couple is also essential. Time spent together can help you maintain a strong bond and support each other emotionally.

Fatherhood is a beautiful journey, but it's not without its challenges. It's crucial to remember that you are not alone in your feelings of self-doubt, anxiety, sleep deprivation, or changes in relationships. Many first-time fathers go through these same experiences.

By taking care of yourself and prioritizing healthy habits, communicating changes in relationships, and asking for help when needed, you can cope with the emotions and thoughts that come with fatherhood. Remember to give yourself grace and enjoy every moment with your little one.

Partner Support And How To Involve The Whole Family In Overcoming Postpartum Depression

As a first-time father, it can be challenging to watch your partner struggle with postpartum depression. It's essential to remember that postpartum depression is not your partner's fault and that there are steps you can take to support her during this challenging time.

Understanding Postpartum Depression

Postpartum depression is a mental health condition that affects many new mothers. It is important to understand the symptoms and identify if your partner is experiencing any of them. Common signs of postpartum depression include:

- Feelings of sadness, hopelessness, or emptiness
- Loss of interest in activities
- Difficulty bonding with your baby
- Changes in appetite and sleep patterns
- Fatigue and loss of energy
- Feelings of guilt and shame

If you think your partner is experiencing postpartum depression, encourage them to contact a medical professional for help.

How to Help Your Partner

There are many ways that you can support your partner as they navigate postpartum depression. Here are a few tips to keep in mind:

- Encourage your partner to seek professional help. Postpartum depression is treatable, and your partner may benefit from working with a therapist or counselor.

- Take on additional household responsibilities. Caring for your partner and new child can be overwhelming, from cooking to cleaning. Helping with household tasks can alleviate some of your partner's stress and pressure.
- Take the time to check in and discuss how they're feeling. Asking about their emotions and thoughts can show that you are there for them and help them feel supported.
- Be mindful of your language. Avoid phrases like "Just snap out of it" or "You're being over dramatic." Postpartum depression is a natural condition and should be treated with care and respect.

Involving the Whole Family

It's essential to involve the whole family in supporting your partner during postpartum depression. Here are a few ways to get others involved:

- Encourage family members and friends to help with household tasks or be available to talk and provide support.
- Create a support network with other new parents in your area. Joining local parent groups or online forums can help connect you to others who understand what you and your partner are going through.
- Make time for family activities that create a sense of connection and help boost mood. Taking walks or playing games together can help alleviate stress and anxiety.

Coping with the Challenges

Watching your partner struggle with postpartum depression can be emotionally challenging. It's crucial to take care of yourself and address any emotional difficulties that you may be experiencing.

- Consider joining a support group for new fathers. Being able to connect with others who are experiencing similar emotions can help create a sense of community and reduce feelings of isolation.

- Take care of your own physical and mental health. Exercise, sleep, and self-care activities can help you cope with stress and reduce the risk of burnout.
- Don't be afraid to seek professional help. Talking with a therapist or counselor can provide you with tools to navigate difficult emotions and reduce toxic thoughts.

Supporting your partner through postpartum depression can be difficult, but it's important to remember that you are not alone. By focusing on open communication, taking care of household tasks, and seeking support from family and friends, you can create a supportive environment for your partner and your growing family to overcome these challenges. Don't forget to take care of yourself along the way and celebrate the small victories.

Chapter 18

Becoming A Confident And Supportive Father

As a first-time father, there is no doubt that you will face challenges and adjustments during this new journey. You may feel anxious about your ability to be a good father or find it difficult to connect with your newborn child. These experiences are normal, and as a fellow father, I understand how challenging this transition can be.

When I became a father for the first time, I sometimes felt uncertain and overwhelmed. However, through my experiences, I've learned that there are ways to become a confident and supportive father. In this chapter, I'll share some key ideas and lessons I've learned, which I hope will help you on your journey.

Remember, fatherhood is a journey; like all journeys, there will be ups and downs. But with the right mindset and a willingness to learn and grow, you can become the father you want to be.

Building A Strong Bond With The New Baby

As the newest addition to your family arrives, you may feel excited, overwhelmed, and even a bit anxious. Creating a bond with your baby is essential to their overall development and well-being.

Importance of Creating a Bond

Your baby's brain is developing rapidly in the first few years of life, and creating a bond with your baby is essential for their growth and social-emotional development. A loving relationship with both parents provides a healthy foundation for your baby to feel secure and form healthy relationships later in life.

Challenges for New Fathers

As a new father, you may experience challenges such as postpartum depression, overwhelming anxiety, or difficulty connecting with your baby. Recognizing and understanding these challenges and taking action to overcome them is essential.

To help you create a strong bond with your baby, here are some practical tips:

1. Provide Comfort and Security

- Hold your baby close: Newborns need to feel close to their parents. Holding them close provides them with the comfort and security that they crave.
- Provide Skin-to-Skin Contact: Skin-to-skin contact is a great way to bond with your baby. When your baby is placed on your chest, it can help regulate their body temperature, breathing, and heart rate.
- Make Eye Contact: Eye contact with your baby helps them establish trust and feel safe in your presence.

2. Interact with Your Baby

- Talk and Sing: Babies love the sound of their parent's voice. Singing or talking to your baby can help their language and brain development.
- Play with Your Baby: Playing with your baby stimulates their senses,

encourages development, and helps develop a strong bond between you and your child.

3. Caregiving

- Diaper Changing: Changing diapers is a bonding experience. It provides you with a chance to spend the time you need with your baby, and it also provides you with moments of intimacy with them.
- Feeding Time: Feeding is an opportunity for bonding with your baby. If your partner is breastfeeding, you can still participate in bonding by giving your baby a bottle of breast milk or formula.
- Bath Time: Bath time is an especially optimal bonding moment between you and your baby. Giving them a warm bath while you softly speak will allow them to recognize and appreciate your nurturing and care.

4. Support your Partner and Share Responsibilities

- It's essential to support your partner and share parenting responsibilities. Make sure to communicate effectively and work together to create a healthy balance.

Building a strong bond with your baby is a process that takes time. By providing comfort and security, interacting with your baby, caregiving, and supporting your partner, you can create a loving and supportive relationship that fosters a lifetime of healthy bond and communication between you and your child.

Nurturing Personal Growth And Taking Care Of Oneself

As you embark on this journey, it's essential to remember that it's not just about taking care of your little one. The truth is, the better you take care of yourself, the better you'll be to care for your child.

Personal growth can easily take a backseat at this stage in your life, but it's crucial to prioritize your well-being. Here are a few lessons I've learned that can help you develop healthy habits, prioritize self-care, and promote positive personal growth:

Lesson 1: Take Care of Your Physical Health

It's natural to be consumed with the demands of being a new dad, but taking care of yourself will positively impact your ability to be a great father. Fuel your body with healthy foods, get enough sleep, and exercise regularly. Being healthy is a gift that you give to yourself and your family.

I was guilty of neglecting my physical health in the early stages of fatherhood. But once I made it a point to exercise regularly and eat healthily, I found that I had more energy and focused to take on the day-to-day responsibilities of fatherhood.

Lesson 2: Take Care of Your Mental Health

Stress, anxiety, and depression are common issues that fathers face. It's essential to recognize that these feelings are normal and that seeking support to manage them is okay.

Find an activity that helps you relax and reduces your stress levels, like meditation or exercise. Prioritize your mental health by taking time for yourself regularly, whether reading a book or walking outside.

Communicating feeling overwhelmed or anxious with your partner, friends, or a mental health professional is also crucial. Remember, seeking help is a sign of strength, not weakness.

Lesson 3: Make Time for Your Hobbies and Interests

Being a dad doesn't mean you have to give up the things you love. Nurturing your hobbies and interests can help you manage stress, improve your mood, and maintain a healthy balance in your life.

Whether it's playing basketball, painting, or working on your car, carving out time for your interests can help you maintain your identity, which is critical for personal growth.

Lesson 4: Seek Out a Support System

Fatherhood can be isolating, especially in the early days when your child requires most of your time and attention. However, you don't have to go through this alone. Building a support system can help you feel connected and supported during this challenging time.

Find other fathers in your community, join a dad's group, or connect with fathers online. Sharing your experiences with other fathers can help normalize feelings and provide valuable insight and support.

Remember, taking care of yourself is not a selfish act. It's a necessary one. Prioritizing physical and mental health, maintaining your hobbies and interests, and building a support system can help you become the best dad possible. Take care of yourself so that you can take care of your child.

Taking An Active Role In Parenting And Childcare

Every first-time father goes through similar struggles, but the good news is that you'll get the hang of it with time and practice.

One of the most vital things you can do as a first-time father is to take an active role in parenting and childcare. Trust me when I say that this is a game-changer. Not only will it help you bond with your child, but it will also help your partner feel supported and less overwhelmed.

Of course, taking an active role in parenting is easier said than done. You're probably juggling work, household responsibilities, and adjusting to your new life as a father. But don't let that stop you. I've been there too, and I can tell you that it's worth the effort.

Here are some practical tips I learned from my trial and error:

Tip 1: Get involved

Changing diapers, giving baths, burping, playing, and feeding are great opportunities for bonding with your child. Plus, it gives your partner a well-deserved break. Don't be afraid of making mistakes. We all do. It's part of the learning process.

Tip 2: Communicate with your partner

Communication is key. Talk with your partner about your new roles, expectations, and how you can support each other. Trust me. You're in this together. Listen to her needs and feelings, and offer your help when necessary.

Tip 3: Don't forget self-care

Parenting is exhausting, so make sure you take care of yourself too. Get enough sleep, eat healthy, and exercise. You can't take care of your child if you don't care for yourself first.

Tip 4: Be present

Your child's first few years are precious, and they grow up fast. Be present and enjoy every moment. Put down your phone, turn off the TV, and engage with your child. Those small moments will make a big difference in the long run.

Now, let's talk about some common mistakes first-time fathers often make. Don't feel ashamed if you've done any of these. We all have, but knowing them can help you avoid them in the future:

Mistake 1: Not asking for help

Parenting can be overwhelming, and it's okay to ask for help. It doesn't make you any less of a father. Talk to your family, friends, or even a professional if needed.

Mistake 2: Expecting your partner to do it all

Parenting is a team effort. Don't expect your partner to do everything on her own. Remember, you're in this together.

Mistake 3: Not being consistent

Children thrive on routines and consistency. Ensure you and your partner are on the same page regarding parenting strategies, rules, and boundaries.

Mistake 4: Not enjoying the moment

Parenting is hard, but it's also rewarding. Don't get so caught up in the challenges you forget to enjoy the joys. Take a step back and appreciate the precious moments with your child.

Taking an active role in parenting and childcare is crucial for your child's development, relationship with your partner, and growth as a father. Remember, you're not alone, and asking for help is okay. Enjoy this new adventure, cherish every moment, and most importantly, be present.

Chapter 19

The Role Of Family And Friends

As a first-time father, you may have noticed that the arrival of your little one has brought your whole family and friend circle together. Everyone is eager to lend a helping hand and cherish each moment with the newest addition to the family.

The chapter covers everything from offering support and guidance to providing care and babysitting. Ink recognizes the significance of having loved ones around and provides invaluable advice on creating a supportive and healthy environment for your child.

Encouraging Family Members To Be A Part Of The Postpartum Care

As a first-time father, feeling overwhelmed with caring for a newborn is normal. However, it's crucial not to let that overshadow the importance of participating actively in postpartum care. Your partner needs you now more than ever, and your involvement in her recovery and your baby's development can make an incredible difference.

It's important to set realistic expectations for yourself and your partner. Don't pressure yourself to be a superhero; try to do everything simultaneously. Instead, communicate with your partner and figure out a plan that works for both of you. Don't hesitate to ask for help from professionals or family members if needed.

Actively listen to your partner's needs and understand that postpartum can be emotionally and physically draining for her. Educate yourself about common postpartum experiences like postpartum depression and how you can be there for her during this difficult time. Encourage her to seek professional help if necessary.

Bonding with your new baby is also important. There are plenty of ways to bond besides just feeding or changing diapers. Try babywearing, giving baths, or reading books together. These bonding experiences will strengthen the relationship between you and your child and make your partner feel supported and appreciated.

Being a supportive partner during postpartum care has countless benefits for your partner and baby. Your presence and involvement can help your partner recover faster and create a closer bond with your child. Remember, being a great father starts from day one. Take an active role in postpartum care, and you'll lay the foundation for a strong and healthy family dynamic.

Be Present

One of the most important things you can do as a new dad is physically and emotionally present. Ensure you are there for your partner and baby as much as possible. This means attending important doctor appointments, staying up during night feeds, and providing emotional support whenever needed.

Offer Practical Help

As a new dad, your partner may be tired and overwhelmed. Offering practical help can go a long way in easing her workload. Offer to take on some of the household chores, cook dinner, or even take care of the baby for a few hours so she can get some rest. These small gestures can make a big difference.

Build Confidence

Becoming a father for the first time can be intimidating, but remember, you're not alone. Don't be afraid to ask for help when you need it, whether from your partner or your friends. You'll also be surprised at how quickly you'll pick up new skills, from changing diapers to soothing a fussy baby. Trust yourself and take it one day at a time.

Be Mindful

Remember that your partner and baby are a team, and their needs should come first. This means being mindful of your partner's physical and emotional needs, as well as the needs of your baby. Communicate openly and honestly with your partner about your feelings and ask for her input on important decisions.

Approach Conflict with Empathy

Conflict is bound to happen, especially when you're both sleep-deprived and stressed. It's important to approach conflict with empathy and under-standing. Try to see things from your partner's perspective and validate her feelings. This doesn't mean you must agree with everything she says, but showing that you understand where she's coming from can help diffuse tension.

Becoming a new father is an exciting and challenging time in your life. Remember that it's okay to feel overwhelmed and that seeking help from your friends and community is a sign of strength, not weakness. You can support your partner and baby during this exciting new chapter of life by being present, offering practical help, building confidence, being mindful, and approaching conflict with empathy.

Differences In Cultural Expectations Of Fathers During Postpartum Period

As a father, you may experience unique cultural and societal expectations during this time. In my experience, navigating cultural expectations as a father during the postpartum period is essential for your well-being and the well-being of your family.

From personal experience and observations, I have learned that different cultures have different expectations of fathers during the postpartum period. For example, in some cultures, fathers are expected to take an active role in caring for the baby and supporting the mother. In contrast, in some cultures, the mother is expected to take full responsibility, and fathers are expected to continue with their work and daily routines, resulting in a smaller role in parenting and supporting the mother.

These cultural and societal expectations can put undue pressure on new fathers during the postpartum period. Fathers who do not conform to these expectations may feel guilty or shamed, creating an emotional strain that could affect their emotional well-being and hinder their ability to support their partner and child.

As a new father, it is essential to understand these cultural expectations and recognize that it is okay not to conform. Instead, focus on what works for you, your partner, and your baby. It's important to communicate with your partner and discuss what role you want to play in caring for the baby and supporting each other. There is no one correct way for a father to behave in the postpartum period.

Navigating cultural expectations may seem overwhelming, but remember, you are not alone. Many fathers fear that they will fail or let their partner and baby down. But parenting is a learning process, and it's okay to make mistakes as long as you learn from them. It is essential to prioritize self-care during this period. Take care of yourself physically and emotionally, allowing you to be present and support your family.

Navigating cultural expectations as a father during the postpartum period can be challenging, but it's crucial for your and your family's well-being.

You can successfully navigate this unique and often precarious time by communicating with your partner, understanding cultural expectations, and prioritizing self-care. Remember, there is no one right way to be a father. You got this!

Importance Of Community Support And Its Benefits

As a new father, you may feel various emotions, from joy and excitement to anxiety and stress. Feeling overwhelmed and needing support for yourself and your partner is okay. In this chapter, I want to share the importance of building a supportive community around you and the benefits of doing so. Community support can help you feel less isolated, reduce stress, and improve your mental health.

There are various types of community support available for new fathers. Online communities such as forums and social media groups can connect you with other fathers going through similar experiences. Parenting groups and workshops provide valuable information and guidance on baby care, parenting, and fatherhood. Mentorship programs can pair you with a seasoned father who can offer advice, support, and guidance.

Building a supportive community can significantly impact your mental health and well-being. By connecting with others, you can reduce feelings of isolation and loneliness, which can be common for new fathers. Additionally, community participation helps you gain new perspectives and insights, improves problem-solving skills, and boosts confidence and self-esteem.

For me, building a supportive community was essential during the post-partum period. I found immense support from a local community of fathers who met regularly to discuss their experiences and offer support. We shared advice, talked about the challenges of fatherhood, and offered each other a listening ear. I also found useful advice and support through online communities, which helped me navigate my new role as a father.

To build a supportive community around you, start by seeking out local parenting groups and workshops in your area. You can also turn to online communities to connect with other fathers. Be open, honest, and vulnerable about your experiences and challenges with other fathers. By sharing your journey with others, you gain support and provide comfort and guidance to fathers going through a similar experience.

As a new father, building a supportive community is essential for your well-being and the well-being of your family. Connecting with other fathers through online and local communities can reduce feelings of isolation and stress, improve your mental health, and gain valuable insights and perspectives. Remember, you are not alone in this journey; support is available.

Chapter 20

Changing Dynamics In Relationship

As a father in the same position, let me tell you that you're not alone. It's normal for couples to go through different stages in their relationship as they navigate the new world of parenthood.

I have learned from my experience and observation that a baby's arrival brings many changes. You'll have to juggle your time between work, family, and your partner, and sometimes finding the right balance can be challenging.

As your little one grows, your attention and focus might be solely on them, leading to a lack of communication and intimacy with your partner. It's essential to remember that your partner is still an important part of your life, and their feelings and needs matter.

In this chapter, we'll dive into the changing dynamics in your relationship with your partner and how you can adapt and thrive together as a family. Remember, being a first-time father is not an easy task, but with the right mindset, support, and guidance, you and your partner can tackle any challenge that comes your way.

Changes In Intimacy And Sex Life During And After Postpartum Period

While you may be overjoyed and feel incredibly grateful for becoming a father, it's important to acknowledge that your relationship with your partner will shift, especially in terms of intimacy and sex life.

During and after childbirth, a woman's body changes significantly. Hormones in her body fluctuate, muscles stretch, and adapting to breastfeeding can be challenging. These changes affect a woman's sexual desire, experiences and can lead to discomfort during sexual activity. For some, it might even take months to resume sexual activity. It's important for you, as a father, to understand and acknowledge these changes.

At this stage, your partner will need your support more than ever. Here are some practical tips and suggestions to help you navigate these changes and maintain intimacy with your partner during this transition period.

Be Patient and Understanding

Your partner's body just went through a monumental change. There were physical and emotional implications that they are still adjusting to. Postpartum recovery is a slow process, and giving her space to heal is important before resuming sexual activity. Remember to communicate and check in regularly to avoid misunderstandings and to ensure you're both on the same page.

Prioritize Intimacy

Intimacy is not just about sex. Hold hands, give each other hugs, and cuddle whenever possible. It creates a deeper bond between you, and your partner can feel more comfortable if you initiate physical contact. It can go a long way in helping your partner feel more comfortable and supported in the postpartum period.

Take it Slow

When you're ready to resume sexual activity, it's essential to take it slow. Start small, and explore each other's bodies without pressure to rush. When intimate, focus on your partner's needs and pleasure. You can also try new things to spice up the process and keep it exciting.

Be Prepared for Challenges

While postpartum sex can be amazing, it can also be challenging. If you experience pain, communicate it with your partner and take a break from intimacy until you're both ready to try again. Be open to trying new things, and don't be afraid to experiment together.

As a new father, it's vital to remember that your relationship with your partner is an integral part of your child's upbringing. Your family will be happier and healthier the more supported and connected your relationship is. The postpartum period is a time of transition, with changes and challenges, but also opportunities for growth and bonding. Patience, communication, and adaptability will help you easily navigate this period. Remember to be kind to yourself and celebrate the experience together.

How To Effectively Communicate Expectations As A Couple

Clear communication and expectations are essential to ensure a healthy relationship as you transition into parenthood. Trust and communication form the backbone of every relationship, and parenthood is no exception. Building trust by being open and honest with each other is essential. Talk about your feelings, your level of preparedness for parenthood, and what kind of support you need from your partner. Listen to your partner's opinions and concerns, and learn to appreciate and respect their point of view.

Setting Mutual Goals

Establishing mutual goals with your partner is crucial in navigating this new phase of life. Communication is key to achieving the goals you set together. Before establishing any goals, it is essential to discuss what is a priority for each person. Agree upon goals that are realistic, achievable, and measurable. Write them down and track your progress together.

Establishing Boundaries

As a new father, your life will change dramatically, and you need to communicate your needs with your partner to establish boundaries. For example, set aside time for yourself, ask for help with tasks, or communicate your need for space. It's important to respect your partner's boundaries and be willing to compromise when necessary.

Handling Conflicts

It is natural to experience conflicts with your partner as you adjust to parenthood. However, it is essential to maintain open communication and listen to each other's concerns. Avoid blame and focus on the issue at hand. Work together to find a mutually agreeable solution. Compromise is the key to resolving conflicts, and it's important to remember that your partner is your support system.

Sharing Responsibilities

Parenthood is a partnership, and sharing the responsibilities ensures the workload is manageable. Communicate with your partner about what needs to be done, establish a schedule, and support each other through the ups and downs. Be mindful of each other's strengths and weaknesses and divide the workload accordingly.

Maintaining Intimacy

As a new father, your focus can quickly shift towards your baby, and it's easy to let intimacy with your partner take a backseat. However, intimacy is essential to sustaining a healthy relationship. Make it a priority to take time for yourselves, connect emotionally, and show affection towards each other.

Recommended Resources

Many resources are available to new fathers that can help them navigate the challenges of parenthood. Consider attending parenting classes, joining online groups or communities, and seeking individual or couples counseling. Additionally, products such as baby carriers, sound machines, and breast-feeding pillows may aid in your journey as a new father.

Parenthood is a new and exciting chapter in your life, filled with challenges and rewards. Communicating effectively with your partner is crucial to navigating this chapter with ease. Remember to build trust, set mutual goals, communicate, establish boundaries, handle conflicts with patience and care, share responsibilities, prioritize intimacy, and avail yourself of helpful resources.

The first thing that comes to mind when you think of your newborn is probably how much love you have for them. Bonding with your baby is crucial during this period. There are a few things you can do to facilitate this process. One thing you can do is to make an effort to hold and cuddle your little one as much as possible. Skin-to-skin contact is great for bonding and can help regulate your baby's temperature and breathing. So, don't hesitate to strip down and hold your baby against your bare chest.

Another important aspect of being a first-time father is supporting your partner. The postpartum period can be physically and emotionally challenging for her, and your support can make a huge difference. It all begins with communication. Talk to your partner and ask her how she is feeling. Listen to her fears, concerns, and frustrations. Your partner is likely to be exhausted, so don't shy away from offering to help with household chores, cooking dinner, or running errands. Little gestures can go a long way in making her feel supported and loved.

Remember that the postpartum period is not just about physical recovery but also hormonal changes and emotional ups and downs. Your partner might experience various emotions, including sadness, anxiety, and irritability. This is all normal as her body and hormones adjust to the new life of motherhood. While seeing your partner go through this can be challenging, remember it's not personal. It's important to be empathetic and patient during this time.

As a first-time father, it's essential to educate yourself on postpartum depression and understand the symptoms. If you notice that your partner is experiencing any of these, such as feeling sad or hopeless, losing interest or pleasure in activities, or having trouble sleeping or eating, encourage her to speak to a healthcare provider. If you need some support, don't hesitate to contact friends or family or seek professional help. Remember that you don't need to go through this alone.

Finally, here are a few tips and tricks to help you navigate this important period in life with empathy and grace:

- Be present: It's easy to get caught up in work or other responsibilities, but try to make an effort to be present and cherish the time you spend with your little one and partner.
- Join parenting groups: Many groups and communities online and offline can offer support and advice for new dads. Don't be afraid to join in on the conversation!
- Take time for yourself: Taking care of yourself is important too. Make time for hobbies, exercise, or just some time to recharge.

Remember, as a first-time dad, you are an important part of your baby's life. You can navigate the postpartum period with confidence and love by being present, supportive, and understanding.

Contributing As An Equal Partner

As a first-time father, you might wonder how to contribute as an equal partner in your child's life. The truth is, there are plenty of ways you can be actively involved and bond with your child that go beyond just changing diapers or giving baths.

One way to bond with your child is through playtime. As your child grows and develops, they will be interested in exploring their surroundings and learning about new things. You can join in on their curiosity and create a safe and playful environment for them to learn and grow. Whether reading books, singing songs, or simply talking and engaging with them, the time you spend bonding with your child can be incredibly rewarding.

Another essential aspect of being an equal partner is supporting your partner. Even though it may not be easy, splitting responsibilities fairly and equally with your partner is important. For example, if your partner has been breastfeeding, you can help by running errands, making meals, or taking care of household chores. By doing so, not only are you taking pressure off of her, but you're also recognizing the importance of her well-being.

It's also important to recognize the significance of self-care during the postpartum period. This can be challenging to do with a newborn, but it's necessary to maintain a healthy and balanced lifestyle. Make time for yourself, whether it's through exercise, getting enough sleep, or just finding some time to do your favorite activities. Remember, taking care of yourself is essential for better engagement with your child and being an equal partner to your spouse.

Forming a community of support can also be crucial for first-time fathers. Look for groups such as new dad support groups or parenting classes in the community. By surrounding yourself with a network of support, you can share your experiences with other dads who might be going through similar challenges. Sharing experiences can provide guidance and validation and help you develop a support system that makes you feel less alone.

Here are some actionable tips to help you feel empowered and prepared for your role as a first-time father:

- Create a routine that works for you and your partner, and stick to it. It can help you manage responsibilities and prevent confusion or frustration.
- Don't be afraid to ask for help. No one can be expected to do everything on their own.
- Take the initiative to learn about your child's development, and find ways to incorporate playtime and engagement that suits your child's interests and needs.
- Be supportive of your partner's decisions and emotions. Recognize their experiences and validate how they feel.
- Remember, being an equal partner means sharing, so find comfortable and sustainable ways to share responsibilities with your spouse and stick to them.

Being an active and equal partner can help create a healthy and meaningful relationship with your child and partner during the postpartum period. Remember, the bond you form with your child and the memories you make during these early years can last a lifetime.

Chapter 21

Raising A Well Rounded Child

As a first-time father, you remember the excitement of holding your little one for the first time. You cherished every moment, from changing their diapers to watching them take their first steps. As your child grows, you realize the importance of being an active and involved parent. You want to provide your child with the best opportunities to learn, grow, and thrive.

Throughout your parenting journey, you have observed that physically active children tend to be happier and have better mental health. They have improved focus, are more confident, and have better self-esteem. Physical activities can also help your child develop stronger social skills and build lasting friendships.

As a father, taking an active role and encouraging your child to be physically active is essential. In this chapter, you will find ways to incorporate physical activities into your daily routine, regardless of your child's age or interests. You'll also learn to overcome common roadblocks, such as screen time and lack of motivation.

Being a Good Role Model for First-Time Fathers

As a first-time father, you want to be the best role model for your child. You want to set a good example, demonstrate positive behavior, and instill values to help your child grow into a responsible, kind, and successful adult. Being a good role model requires effort and intentionality, but it is a crucial aspect of parenting.

Being Present and Engaged

One of the most important ways to be a good role model is by being present and engaged in your child's life. This means actively participating in their hobbies, interests, and schoolwork. It also means putting down your phone, turning off the TV, and giving your child attention.

Show your child that they are a priority in your life by scheduling quality time together, whether playing catch in the park or reading a bedtime story. Being present and engaged demonstrates the value of spending time with loved ones and building strong relationships.

Demonstrating Responsibility

Another important aspect of being a good role model is demonstrating responsibility. This means taking care of yourself and your family, fulfilling your obligations, and being accountable for your actions.

Show your child that responsibility is a positive trait by following through with your commitments, paying bills on time, and making healthy choices. Your child is watching and learning from your actions, so modeling responsible behavior is important.

Practicing Honesty and Kindness

Honesty and kindness are essential values to instill in your child, starting with modeling these behaviors yourself. Be honest with your child, even if it means admitting your mistakes.

Model kindness by showing empathy for others and treating people with respect. Demonstrate generosity by volunteering in your community or donating time or resources to causes you care about. Your child will learn from your actions and develop a sense of compassion and altruism.

Setting Healthy Boundaries

Setting healthy boundaries is also important to be a good role model. By maintaining your boundaries and respecting others, you are modeling healthy relationships. Demonstrate self-respect by setting boundaries in your personal and professional life. Teach your child to do the same by respecting their boundaries and modeling healthy communication.

Being a good role model takes intentionality and effort, but it is critical to raising a well-rounded child. Being present, responsible, honest, kind, and boundary-aware sets your child up for success and help them develop strong values and a positive outlook on life.

Advancing Emotional Intelligence Of The Child

Emotional intelligence is an essential skill that helps children navigate social interactions, regulate their emotions, and develop healthy relationships. As an educator or child development expert, you can help children advance their emotional intelligence by incorporating the following strategies into their daily lives.

Name That Emotion

Teach children to identify and name their emotions. Young children can benefit from learning basic emotions such as happy, sad, angry, or frustrated. Encourage older children to identify more complex emotions such as disappointment, embarrassment, or jealousy.

Practice Mindfulness

Mindfulness activities can help children develop self-awareness and self-regulation skills. Encourage children to take a few deep breaths, pause, and notice their feelings in the present moment. Guided breathing exercises, deep relaxation techniques, or yoga can also be effective.

Engage in Role-Playing

Role-playing can be fun and useful to help children develop empathy and interpersonal relationships. Use puppets, dolls, or imaginary scenarios to encourage children to put themselves in another's shoes and express their feelings.

Keep a Feelings Journal

Encourage children to keep a journal of their emotions. Writing down their feelings can help them develop self-awareness and regulate their emotions. It can also help them identify patterns in their emotional responses and recognize triggers.

Use Positive Language

Positive language can help children develop a growth mindset and a positive outlook. Encourage children to use phrases such as "I can try again" or "I am learning" instead of negative self-talk that can hinder emotional growth.

Develop Empathy Cards

Empathy cards are a fun and interactive way for children to practice empathy. Create cards with different emotions and scenarios, and encourage children to pick a card and share how they would feel in that situation.

Use Storytelling

Storytelling can help children identify and express a range of emotions. Use age-appropriate books or create your own stories to help children relate to characters, identify emotions, and explore different perspectives.

Integrating these strategies into existing programs or using them at home can help children advance their emotional intelligence. Children with strong emotional intelligence skills are better equipped to navigate social interactions, manage stress, and build healthy relationships. We can help children become empathetic, mindful, and compassionate individuals by fostering emotional intelligence.

Encouraging Diversity And Gender-Inclusiveness Among Children

Encouraging diversity and gender-inclusiveness in young children is essential for building a more vibrant and inclusive society. Education is the foundation for promoting inclusivity and diversity, and it should start with children from birth. We'll explore practical tips and strategies for promoting diversity and gender-inclusiveness among young children.

The Importance of Early Education

Early education plays a crucial role in shaping children's worldviews. Young children are highly impressionable and absorb information effortlessly. It's never too early to promote acceptance of diversity, including differences in gender, ethnicity, race, religion, and more. Introducing children to diverse cultures and teaching tolerance helps children understand and appreciate differences.

Diverse Representation in Children's Media

Children's media provides a rich opportunity to promote diversity and inclusivity. Children's books should depict or represent a variety of races, cultures, and ethnicity. In addition, children's media should also depict traditional gender roles positively and progressively. Parents should avoid traditional gender stereotypes or labels and expose children to activities that help break gender norms.

The Role of Parents and Caregivers

Parents and caregivers play a significant role in shaping children's views of diversity and inclusivity. Parents should create an environment that celebrates differences and values diversity. Simple adjustments like creating a diverse toy chest or ensuring children's activities are free from gender stereotypes can help foster inclusivity.

The Benefits of Cross-Cultural Learning

Cross-cultural learning helps children understand and appreciate differences and promotes inclusion. Children can learn about other cultures and practice acceptance by attending cultural events or bartering with international friends. Parents can help promote active inclusion by seeking diverse community events or organizing exchanges with families from different cultural backgrounds.

Suggestions and Resources for Parents and Educators

Education on diversity and inclusivity is a lifelong journey for children. Parents and educators can positively impact children by providing access to diverse authors, media, and toys and actively exploring other cultures as a family. Additionally, parents and educators should teach children to respect diverse beliefs, traditions, and ways of life.

Promoting diversity and gender inclusivity among young children requires intentionality and a willingness to expose them to a broader world than their immediate social and cultural surroundings. There are many opportunities to promote inclusivity and diversity for young children, from diverse books to multicultural festivals. Parents, caregivers, and educators are crucial in giving children the tools to become accepting, open-minded adults.

Managing Screen Time

Being a first-time father in the digital age can be challenging, especially when managing your child's screen time. Monitoring their use while still keeping them engaged and entertained is tough. But don't worry; you're not alone. We've all been there!

Start Early

It's important to start early when managing your child's screen time. You can begin setting limits on-screen use at two or three. Create a schedule with designated times when screens are allowed so your child knows when to use them appropriately.

Create Tech-Free Zones

Designate specific areas in your home as tech-free zones, such as the dinner table or bedroom. Encourage your child to engage in reading, coloring, or outdoor activities.

Monitor and Set Limits

Be aware of the apps your child uses, and set time limits for screen use accordingly. Encourage your child to take breaks regularly while using screens, whether it be taking a walk or playing outside.

Lead by Example

As a father, set an example for your child by limiting screen time for yourself. Show the importance of balance by engaging in activities such as playing board games, reading, or spending time with your child without screens as a distraction.

Use Parental Controls

Technology allows us to set limits and monitor our child's screen time through parental controls. Take advantage of these tools to check your child's screen time.

The Power of Conversation

Engage in conversation with your child about why it's important to have limitations regarding screen time. Explain the importance of personal connection and outdoor playtime.

Personal Insights

As a father of four, I found it helpful to have a designated time every week when the family had no screens; we would play games, spend time outside or engage in other activities that fostered family connections. Even now that my kids are older, we still try to have a day without screens, which they enjoy.

Managing your child's screen time is essential to parenting in the digital age. You can ensure your child develops healthy media habits by implementing simple strategies such as creating tech-free zones, using parental controls, and leading by example. Remember to communicate with your child and set realistic limits for your family's lifestyle. With some experimentation, you'll figure out the right balance that works for everyone.

Chapter 22

The Working Dads

As a first-time father, the process and experience of juggling work and family may be challenging. As a working dad, you might struggle to balance work-life and family time. In this chapter, you will review several effective ways to navigate the challenges of balancing work and family life.

Balancing Work and Family

One of the most significant challenges of working dad is that you may miss important moments in your child's life. Due to work commitments, you may miss your child's first step, recital, or school show. Talking to your employer about family obligations is essential to determine the best way forward.

Speaking to your partner and determining how to balance your parental responsibilities is important. For instance, you could decide to alternate drop-offs and pick-ups from school or manage daycare drop-offs if that is an option. If you have an understanding employer, consider working from home, which is becoming a norm, especially with the world becoming more digitalized.

Personal Experiences

As a working father, one of the most inspiring things is to witness your child grow and learn new things. You will have moments where you feel like you are doing an excellent job at parenting and others that leave you feeling defeated. Sometimes, you may feel like you're not balancing family and work as well as you should, but it's important to understand that you are doing your best. Over time, you'll get into the rhythm of balancing and spend more quality time with your family.

Remember that it's okay to make mistakes. Acknowledge your limitations, but never lose sight of your priorities. The most important thing to remember is to spend quality time with your child, build memories, and cherish every moment you get with them. To sum it up, make parenting a partnership with your partner, carefully manage your time at work and home, adjust when necessary, and hang in there. You got this.

Paternity Leave: Taking Time Off to Bond with Your Newborn

The need to return to work soon after the birth can be daunting. Many fathers might feel guilty or ashamed for wanting to miss work and take time off with their newborn. However, it is essential to know that taking paternity leave can benefit you and your child.

In America, you are entitled to up to 12 weeks of unpaid leave under the Family Medical Leave Act (FMLA). Some states may offer paid leave, and private companies may have policies that give additional benefits. It is essential to speak to your employer to find out more information.

Paternity leave allows you to bond with your newborn during their early developmental stages. These early stages are critical in establishing a strong bond between you and your child. Paternity leave also allows you to be more involved in their care, such as feedings, diaper changes, and other important milestones that may otherwise be missed.

Taking time off from work may seem like a difficult decision, but it is essential to remember that your newborn needs you as much as you need them. Paternity leave can ease the transition into fatherhood, reduce stress and anxiety, and create an opportunity to have uninterrupted time with your child.

Some companies put a stigma on men for taking paternity leave. However, it is your legal right, and companies cannot lawfully discriminate against fathers who choose to take paternity leave. Knowing that you are setting a good example and promoting discussions around more father-friendly workplace policies by taking paternity leave is essential.

Taking paternity leave is a decision that should never be taken lightly. It can be an opportunity to create an unbreakable bond with your newborn and help you transition into fatherhood smoothly. Don't feel ashamed or embarrassed about taking paternity leave. It is your right as an American citizen to do so, and it's a decision that may benefit both you and your family in the long run.

The Advantages of FMLA and Paternity Leave for New Fathers

The Family and Medical Leave Act (FMLA) is a federal law that provides eligible employees with up to 12 weeks of unpaid leave per year for specific reasons, including the birth or adoption of a child. FMLA allows fathers to take time off work to bond with their newborn child without worrying about losing their job or health benefits.

Paternity leave is a type of FMLA leave that allows fathers to take time off work to care for their newborn or newly adopted child. Some companies provide paid paternity leave, while others offer unpaid leave, and some states have their paternity leave laws.

There are numerous benefits to taking advantage of FMLA and paternity leave. The most crucial benefit is bonding with your newborn child during their crucial developmental stage. Paternity leave allows you to be more involved in your child's care, including feedings, diaper changes, and other essential parenting responsibilities.

Moreover, paternity leave enables fathers to support postpartum mothers, and it has been found that fathers who take paternity leave experience fewer postpartum depression symptoms than those who do not. Paternity leave also helps fathers develop a more profound sense of connection and attachment to their children, which is essential for healthy child development and can increase fathers' parenting confidence.

Approaching Employers About Paternity Leave

Approaching employers about paternity leave can be a daunting prospect for many fathers. However, most employers must comply with FMLA regulations, and taking paternity leave is entirely legal. It is essential to communicate effectively with your employer about your leave and to provide as much notice as possible before taking it.

Making the Most of Your Leave

After securing paternity leave, making the most of that time is essential. You can use the time to bond with your newborn child, support the postpartum mother, and care for your physical and emotional health. Consider creating a plan for your leave to help you balance your parenting duties and priorities and resist the urge to work in your free time during your leave.

Taking advantage of FMLA and paternity leave can be a lifesaver for new dads. Paternity leave allows fathers to bond with their newborn child and support the postpartum mother, laying the foundation for stable family dynamics. Do not feel guilty or ashamed about taking paternity leave. It is your legal right as a father and benefits you and your family in the long run.

Balancing Work and Home Life: Strategies for New Fathers

Congratulations on becoming a new dad! Balancing work and family life can be a challenging experience. Still, with the right strategies and mindset, it is possible to be a successful and involved parent while meeting work expectations. In this chapter, I share my experiences and observations on managing work expectations and communication strategy as a new father, providing practical tips and strategies that help you balance work and home life.

As a new father, you may experience many challenges as you balance work and family life. You might feel nervous about discussing your family obligations with your employer or worried about not being there for your child's key moments. You may also face pressure to meet work expectations while being a present and involved dad.

Acknowledging and understanding these challenges is important to help manage them effectively.

Communicating with Your Employer

Effective communication is key to balancing work and home life. Be open and honest with your employer about your needs and expectations as a new father. Find out what options are available to help you balance work and family life, such as flexible work arrangements or paternity leave.

Also, stay proactive about communication. Keep your employer updated about any changes in your family life or schedule, and ensure they know your priorities and commitments outside of work.

Communicating with Your Partner

Effective communication with your partner is also important. Balance your partner's expectations while also managing your work expectations. You can divide work and family responsibilities equally or alternate them. Speak honestly about each other's priorities, stresses, and challenges for the week, and make a plan so that neither of you feels overwhelmed.

Setting Expectations and Boundaries

Setting clear expectations and boundaries is key to achieving work-life balance as a new father. You might consider setting a strict time limit with your employer, during which they can contact you outside of work hours. Or, you might set specific days or times during which you are dedicated to spending time with your family without interruptions from work.

It is also essential to set realistic expectations for yourself. Understand that balancing work and home life can be challenging, and asking for help when needed is okay. Delegate work when possible, but create a to-do list for later to ensure that work doesn't consume the entire day.

Balancing work and home life is a challenge that many new fathers face. However, effective communication, setting clear expectations and boundaries, and being honest with your employer and partner makes it possible to be a successful parent while meeting work expectations. Being proactive and willing to ask for help can also prevent burnout and maintain a healthy balance between work and home life.

Embracing Flexible Work Arrangements

As you navigate the challenges of adjusting to parenthood, embracing flexible work arrangements is important. In this section, I'll explain why flexible work arrangements are essential for new fathers and provide tips and guidance on communicating effectively with employers and balancing work and family responsibilities.

The Benefits of Flexible Work Arrangements

Your priorities and responsibilities have shifted. Your family is now your top priority, but you still need to meet your work responsibilities. Flexible work arrangements provide a way to balance both. There are numerous benefits to embracing flexible work arrangements. Here are just a few:

- Reduced Stress: Flexible work arrangements allow you to balance your work and home life, reducing stress and creating a more positive work–life balance.
- Increased Productivity: Studies have shown that flexible work arrangements can increase productivity by allowing workers to focus on their work when they're most productive.
- Improved Job Satisfaction: When you feel like you have control over your work schedule and can meet your family responsibilities, it can make for a happier and more motivated employee.
- Enhanced Health and Well-being: Without the stress of juggling work and family obligations, you'll have more time to take care of yourself, leading to better health and well-being.

Communicating with your employer is key to negotiating flexible work arrangements. Here are some tips for how to do it effectively:

- Be clear and direct: Explain why you need a flexible work arrangement without being unsure.
- Provide specific examples of how it will benefit them: For example, mention that you'll be able to work more efficiently or that it would be more cost-effective.
- Be open to compromise: If your employer can't meet your exact needs, be open to finding a solution that works for both of you.
- Be prepared to discuss how you'll be able to manage your responsibilities: This includes outlining how you'll manage your work schedule, what you'll need to do to be productive, and how you'll manage any childcare

responsibilities.

Creating a Flexible Work Arrangement that Works for You

There are many flexible work arrangements to choose from.

Flex-Hours

You can vary your work hours with flex hours to meet your family obligations. For example, you could start the day early and finish early or work a compressed workweek.

- Communicate your schedule: Be clear about when you'll be available to work so your employer can plan accordingly.
- Set realistic expectations: Understand that working different hours from your colleagues can be challenging and ensure everyone knows your availability.

Remote Work

Remote work options allow you to work from home or another location. This can be especially helpful if you have young children at home and must be present for their care.

- Create a designated workspace: Set up a separate area for work to help you minimize distractions and stay focused.
- Stay connected: Ensure you are easily accessible to your employer and colleagues through email, phone, video conferencing, or a chat app.

Child Care Benefits

Some employers offer childcare benefits, such as on-site childcare or subsidies for childcare costs.

- Understand the benefits: Be clear about what childcare benefits your employer offers and how they can be used.
- Plan: Coordinate your work schedule around your childcare responsibilities.

Finding Work-Life Balance

Negotiating flexible work arrangements is just the first step to finding work-life balance. Here are some additional tips:

- Set boundaries: Be sure to carve out time for yourself and your family. For example, make sure that you have at least one night a week dedicated to spending time with your family without interruptions from work.
- Stay organized: Create a schedule and to-do list to keep track of your work and personal commitments.
- Be kind to yourself: Understand that balancing work and family responsibilities can be challenging, and permit yourself to ask for help when needed.

Transitioning to parenthood can be a challenge. Embracing flexible work arrangements can help you balance your work and family responsibilities effectively, reduce stress, enhance productivity, and improve job satisfaction. Communicating effectively with your employer, creating arrangements that work for you, and finding work-life balance are all essential for success. With the right strategies and mindset, you can enjoy the benefits of flexible work arrangements while being a present and involved father.

Chapter 23

Guiding the New Generation

As a parent, your role is to help your child grow and develop, equipping them with the tools they need to thrive in a rapidly changing world. This means helping them adapt and evolve with the environment and society, channeling their creativity, managing anxiety, and disciplining them with love, understanding, and kindness. In this chapter, we'll explore these topics in-depth and provide practical tips and advice to help you guide the new generation.

Helping Your Child Adapt and Evolve With the Environment and Society

Adapting and evolving with the environment and society is crucial for future success. Here's how you can help your child develop these skills:

Encourage curiosity

Encourage your child to be curious and to ask questions. This helps them develop the critical thinking and problem-solving skills needed to navigate a changing world.

Foster a growth mindset

Teach your child that their abilities and intelligence can be developed with hard work and effort and that failures are opportunities to grow and learn.

Teach them to be flexible

Teach your child to be flexible and adaptable. This means exposing them to new experiences and challenges, encouraging them to try new things, and engage with different perspectives.

Model resilience

Be a role model for resilience, showing your child how to bounce back from setbacks, handle stress, and stay positive.

Channeling Creativity in Kids and Managing Anxiety to Achieve It

Encouraging creativity is essential for children's mental and emotional health. Here are some ways to channel your child's creativity while helping them manage anxiety:

Create a safe and supportive environment

Create a safe and supportive environment that encourages your child to express their feelings and creativity without fear of judgment or criticism.

Provide opportunities for creative expression

Provide your child with opportunities for creative expression, such as drawing, painting, writing, or music.

Show an interest in their creations

Show an interest in your child's creative pursuits, and ask them questions about what they are creating to help them develop their skills and boost their confidence.

Teach them to manage anxiety

Teach your child techniques to manage anxiety, such as deep breathing, mindfulness, and positive self-talk.

The Importance of Disciplining with Love, Understanding, and Kindness

Discipline is essential to parenting, but it's important to do it effectively and with kindness. Here's how:

Set clear expectations

Set clear expectations for your child's behavior early on and provide positive reinforcement for good behavior.

Avoid harsh punishments

Avoid harsh punishments like spanking or yelling. Instead, use consequences that are appropriate for the situation, such as taking away privileges or extra chores.

Use positive reinforcement

Use positive reinforcement to encourage good behavior. Praise your child when they do well, and give them incentives to continue behaving well.

Practice active listening

Active listening can help you understand your child's perspective and avoid misunderstandings leading to discipline problems.

Guiding the new generation is no easy task, but you can help your child thrive in a rapidly changing world with patience, love, understanding, and kindness. Encourage curiosity, foster a growth mindset, teach them to be flexible and resilient, encourage creativity, and discipline with kindness. With these skills, your child will be equipped to adapt and evolve with the environment and society, navigate anxiety, and achieve success.

Empowering Your Child to Succeed

In addition to helping your child adapt and evolve, channeling their creativity, and disciplining with kindness, there are other ways you can empower your child to succeed:

Encouraging a love of learning is crucial for your child's academic and personal success. Here's how you can foster a love of learning in your child:

Teach your child that learning is fun

Make learning fun by playing educational games, reading together, listening to music, or watching educational shows.

Support their interests

Support your child's interests by providing books, materials, and opportunities to practice and explore their passions.

Encourage independent thinking

Encourage your child to think independently by asking them open-ended questions, listening to their responses without judgment, and helping them develop their analytical, problem-solving, and decision-making skills.

Developing Positive Relationships

Developing positive relationships is essential for your child's social and emotional development. Here's how to help your child build positive relationships:

Model good relationship skills

Model good relationship skills by treating those around you with kindness, compassion, and respect.

Teach them about empathy

Teach your child empathy, understanding, and connecting with others' emotions.

Encourage positive communication

Encourage positive communication by teaching your child how to listen actively, express their needs and emotions clearly and respectfully, and resolve conflicts constructively.

Building Confidence

Building confidence is vital for your child's self-esteem and success. Here's how to help your child build confidence:

Acknowledge their successes

Acknowledge your child's successes, no matter how small they may be. This can help motivate and reinforce positive behavior.

Encourage them to take risks

Encourage your child to take risks, try new things, and step outside their comfort zones.

Provide opportunities for autonomy

Provide opportunities for your child to make choices and exercise autonomy. This can help build confidence, independence, and decision-making skills.

Guiding the new generation is a complex and rewarding task. By helping your child adapt and evolve, channeling their creativity, disciplining with kindness, encouraging a love of learning, developing positive relationships, and building confidence, you can set them up for success in all areas of their life. Remember, empowering your child to succeed is not just about giving them the tools to tackle the challenges they will face but also about being supportive and loving in their life.

The Role of Parents in Nurturing Children's Social Skills and Emotional Intelligence

As a parent, you play a crucial role in nurturing your child's social skills and emotional intelligence (EQ). Social skills and EQ are essential for building healthy relationships, managing emotions, and navigating the social world. Here are some ways to help your child develop these skills:

Fostering Social Skills

Encouraging Interaction with Peers

Encourage your child to spend time with peers and socialize in different settings. This can include participating in teams, clubs, or after-school activities.

Practicing Communication Skills

Practice communication skills with your child, such as active listening, expressing opinions and emotions, and using appropriate body language.

Role-playing Social Situations

Role-play social situations with your child, such as sharing, taking turns, or asking for help. This can help them build empathy, perspective-taking, and compromise skills.

Teaching Social Norms

Teach your child social norms, such as using manners, respecting others' boundaries, and showing empathy. This can help them build a sense of responsibility, social awareness, and self-discipline.

Developing Emotional Intelligence

Teaching Emotional Regulation

Teach your child how to recognize and regulate emotions constructively. This can include deep breathing, mindfulness techniques, or self-soothing strategies.

Modeling Positive Emotions

Model positive emotions and social behaviors, such as gratitude, kindness, and forgiveness. This can help your child build empathy, optimism, and positive self-image.

Encouraging Introspection

Encourage your child to reflect on their emotions and behavior, such as identifying strengths and areas for growth, setting achievable goals, and learning from mistakes.

Building Resilience

Help your child develop resilience, the ability to bounce back from setbacks or challenges. This can include building coping strategies, enhancing self-esteem, or fostering social support.

As a parent, you can shape your child's social and emotional well-being. By fostering social skills and EQ, you can help your child build healthy relationships, manage emotions, and navigate social situations confidently and gracefully. Remember to model positive behaviors and emotions, communicate effectively, and provide opportunities for reflection, growth, and resilience. With your guidance and support, your child can thrive and succeed in all areas of their life.

Conclusion

Becoming a dad for the first time can be overwhelming.

This book has provided a comprehensive guide for new dads - from learning about what to expect in their newborn's behavior and development to understanding their parenting style and creating their plan for success.

New dads have been equipped with transferable skills to handle any situation with their newborn, like swaddling, burping, and comfort measures.

They also now understand the importance of self-care - for them and their babies - and how it can impact the family dynamic. Becoming a parent is an incredible journey that starts with your newborn's first cries and lasts beyond infancy. New fathers can confidently prepare for this amazing adventure with this newfound knowledge.

Considering the information and advice presented in this book, new dads can feel empowered as they enter their new role. With patience, understanding, and dedication to self-care, becoming a dad can be an exciting and rewarding experience full of joy and love. With this knowledge, fathers can look forward to all that lies ahead as they embark on their parenting journey.

With a little preparation and understanding, new dads can face the adventure of being a father with confidence and optimism. Congratulations on becoming a dad! The best is yet to come!

The key points covered in this book are how to help nurture children's social skills and emotional intelligence as a parent. This includes fostering social skills by encouraging peer interaction, practicing communication skills, role-playing social situations, and teaching social norms.

Parents should focus on developing emotional intelligence by teaching emotional regulation, modeling positive emotions, encouraging introspection, and building resilience. With the right guidance and support from parents, children can be empowered to succeed in all areas of their life.

Parents must remember that these skills take time to develop and require patience and understanding. By providing a supportive environment where your child feels safe to express themselves and explore, you can help them learn and grow as individuals. Fostering social skills and emotional intelligence can be a rewarding experience for parents and children. It is an essential part of a child's overall development that will support them throughout their lives.

Postpartum care is essential for fathers and families alike. Fathers have a unique role in the postpartum period, offering physical and emotional support that can make all the difference in helping new mothers adjust to their changing roles as parents. As such, dads-to-be must be informed about what they can do during this transition to prepare them when the baby arrives.

Families should ensure that both mother and father receive adequate postpartum care by seeking professional help. With proper knowledge and understanding of the importance of postpartum care for fathers and families, we can create an environment where everyone involved feels supported through this life stage change—and ultimately thrive together afterward!

Knowing your unique role during the postpartum period is important as a father-to-be. With proper knowledge and understanding, you can provide physical and emotional support that will impact your family's health. This includes encouraging fathers to seek help and support when needed, such as speaking to a professional, participating in postpartum groups, and/or seeking support from friends, family, and other parents.

Fathers need to take care of their emotional health as well. This could include regular exercise, dieting, meditation, and positive affirmations, which can help manage stress levels while promoting overall mental well-being. By understanding the importance of postpartum care for fathers and families alike, we can ensure that everyone involved will benefit during this time of transition—and beyond! Postpartum care is essential for both mothers and fathers alike.

During this period of transition and change, both parents must receive adequate emotional and physical support so they are best able to cope with the demands of parenthood. Fathers should be encouraged to seek help and support when needed, such as speaking to a professional, participating in postpartum groups, and/or seeking support from friends, family, and other parents. Fathers also need to take care of their emotional health by engaging in regular exercise, dieting, meditation, and positive affirmations, which can help manage stress levels while promoting overall mental well-being.

By providing families with the resources they need during this period of change, we can ensure that both mothers and fathers are equipped with the skills required to embrace the joys—and challenges—of parenthood together.

Parenting is a lifelong journey filled with ups and downs. As parents, nurturing our children's emotional intelligence and social skills is important to raise well-rounded, socially aware individuals.

References

American Pregnancy Association. (2015). *Hormonal Changes After Pregnancy*. Retrieved from https://americanpregnancy.org/first-year-of-life/hormonal-changes-after-pregnancy-6801/ (accessed on January 8, 2023).

American Psychological Association. (2020). *Postpartum Depression*. Retrieved from https://www.apa.org/pi/women/resources/reports/postpartum-depression (accessed on February 2, 2023).

National Institute of Mental Health. (2018). *Postpartum Depression Facts*. Retrieved from https://www.nimh.nih.gov/health/publications/postpartum-depression-facts/index.shtml (accessed on March 1, 2023).

American College of Obstetricians and Gynecologists. (2018). *Postpartum Care*. Retrieved from https://www.acog.org/womens-health/faqs/postpartum-care (accessed on January 15, 2023).

National Health Service. (n.d.). *Your post-pregnancy body*. Retrieved from https://www.nhs.uk/conditions/baby/support-and-services/your-post-pregnancy-body/ (accessed on January 22, 2023).

Mental Health America. (2019). *Postpartum Depression & Anxiety*. Retrieved from https://www.mhanational.org/postpartum-depression-and-anxiety (accessed on February 12, 2023).

Psych Central. (n.d.). *Why Feeling Left Out Stings + 8 Healthy Ways to Cope.* Retrieved from https://psychcentral.com/blog/why-feeling-left-out-stings-8-healthy-ways-to-cope (accessed on March 8, 2023).

Science of People. (n.d.). *Feeling Left Out By Your Friends? 9 Tips to Overcome It.* Retrieved from https://www.scienceofpeople.com/feeling-left-out/ (accessed on February 15, 2023).

Ashley Hudson Therapy. (n.d.). *What To Do When You Feel Left Out.* Retrieved from https://www.ashleyhudsontherapy.com/what-to-do-when-you-feel-left-out/ (accessed on March 22, 2023).

Additional Resources

Several resources are available to fathers seeking support in the postpartum period, including books, blogs, and online communities.

Books

Many books provide detailed advice and tips on how fathers can best support their partners postpartum. These include "The Essential Guide for New Dads" by Armin Brott, "The New Father: A Dad's Guide to the First Year" by Armin Brott and Jennifer Ash, and "From Dude to Dad: The Diaper Dude Guide to Pregnancy" by Chris Pegula. Various parenting guidebooks written specifically for dads cover topics from birth through infancy.

Information On Seeking Professional Help For Postpartum Depression And Anxiety

1. Postpartum Support International: https://www.postpartum.net/
2. Anxiety and Depression Association of America: https://adaa.org/
3. Mental Health America: http://www.mentalhealthamerica.net/conditions/postpartum-depression
4. The National Perinatal Association: https://nationalperinatalassociation.org/resources/ppdanswers
5. American Psychological Association - Find a Therapist Tool: http://locator.apa.org/?_ga=2.251883191.1386099444.1543348849-555046552
6. Psychology Today - Find a Therapist Tool: https://therapists.psycholo

gytoday.com/rms/

7. The National Women's Health Information Center: https://www.womenshealth.gov/mental-health

8. Pubmed Article on Postpartum Depression Treatment Options: https://www.ncbi.nlm.nih.gov/pmc/articles/PMC3011048/

9. National Alliance on Mental Illness: http://www.nami.org/Find-Support/Family-Members-and-Caregivers/Postpartum-Depression

10. Baby Blues Connection: https://www.babybluesconnection.org/postpartum_depression_resources.htm

11. Postpartum Progress Support Groups: http://www.postpartumprogress.org/support-groups-for-moms-with-postpartum-depression/

12. American College of Obstetricians and Gynecologists (ACOG): https://www.acog.org/Patients/FAQs/Depression-During-and-After-Pregnancy

13. BetterHelp: Online counseling and therapy with licensed professional counselors, therapists, psychologists, social workers, and psychiatrists via text messaging, video chat, or phone.

14. Talkspace: Therapy by licensed professionals through their secure platform that can help individuals work on specific issues such as depression or stress management.

15. Amwell: Online healthcare with board-certified doctors from various specialties who can diagnose and treat many health conditions, including anxiety and depression.

16. MDLive: Virtual care services for mental health provided by experienced behavioral health providers available 24/7 in all 50 states

17. Ginger Mental Health Care: Evidence-based psychotherapy with access to both individual sessions in real-time as well as self-guided digital programs that feature assessments, worksheets, videos, and resources tailored to patient's needs

18. Livehealth Online Mental Health Services: Access to Board Certified Psychiatrists providing personalized care through quick virtual visits using a smartphone app or computer

About the Author

Jack Ink is a writer, adventurer, and first-time dad. When he's not changing diapers or singing lullabies to his newborn son, he's probably off on some wild adventure.

Born and raised in the heart of the Rocky Mountains, Jack always had a love for the outdoors and a spirit of adventure. He spent his younger years exploring the wilderness, climbing mountains, and rafting down raging rivers.

But when he became a first-time dad, Jack's sense of adventure took on a new meaning. He quickly learned that being a dad is the greatest adventure of all, with all the highs and lows that come with it.

From sleepless nights to his first words and steps, Jack has found joy and inspiration in every moment of fatherhood. He's learned to embrace the chaos, laugh at the messy moments, and cherish the precious time spent with his son.

Jack still manages to squeeze in some adventures in his spare time, from taking his son on her first camping trip to exploring new hiking trails with a baby carrier on his back.

Jack knows that being a first-time dad is not always easy, but he's found that the rewards are more than worth it. He's grateful for the opportunity to share his experiences with other new dads and hopes to inspire them to embrace the adventure of fatherhood.

Made in the USA
Middletown, DE
17 September 2024

60497189R00144